HOW TO GET MORE

Love,
Money,
and
Success

by Traveling on Your Birthday

Bob Marks

JOVE
PRESS

Printed in the U.S.A.
ISBN 978-0-9821691-0-0

Jove Press
420 E. 80th Street, Suite 10G
New York City, NY 10075
www.bobmarksastrologer.com

Acknowledgements

First and foremost, I would like to thank Diane Cramer for advice, comments, and editing. Thanks also to Patricia Konigsberg for her invaluable help and support. And last, but not least, a multitude of thanks to my favorite niece, Terry Marks, who not only is responsible for the fabulous design, but also banged the book into shape and kicked my butt daily until the project was at the printers.

I was one of several astrologers who independently discovered that horoscopes could be changed by traveling on your birthday. The first astrologer to do this was Ray Merriman who published the technique in 1977. I came up with the same idea independently in 1981 and didn't find Ray's book until 1989. So Ray takes first place. However, he doesn't use precession-corrected charts. I do because they work better. The evidence is presented in the book that follows.

Thanks also to the clients for sharing their stories. The names have been changed, but the events are accurate, and the results of their travels were as they related them to me.

Contents

Part I

INTRODUCTION

Part II

THE RULES

Part III

HOW WELL DOES THIS WORK?

APPENDIX

What the Planets Mean in Return Charts

Preface

In 1981, I traveled on my birthday. That year, my income more than doubled. I've been traveling on my birthday ever since. I've also sent clients on thousands of birthday trips. The results are frequently dramatic. This book will show you how to travel to the right place on your birthday to improve any area of your life that you want.

Why did I travel to begin with? What possible reason could there be for thinking that being in another place on your birthday could make any difference at all in what happens for the rest of the year?

In astrology, one of the forecasting techniques is the *solar return*. Every year, on your birthday, the Sun "returns" to the place it occupied when you were born. If you make a chart for the exact time of the return, that is your solar return horoscope, or as I call it, your *birthday horoscope*. Like any astrology chart, the solar return depends on the location as well as the time. The obvious question then for any astrologer is: Can you change your life by traveling on your birthday? Yes, of course you can. Otherwise I wouldn't be writing this book!

Please note, these interpretations are for return, not natal charts. While there is a great similarity between the interpretations, there are also important differences. In a return chart, the effect is only for a particular time period. A natal chart is for life, which gives a lot of time to make adjustments.

This book is not a beginners guide to astrology. The introduction will give you some basics, and you can also go to my website:

www.bobmarksastrologer.com/TOClessons.htm

There are over 200 pages of lessons there and they are free. (I got tired of having to explain to people that there is more to astrology than 12 Sun Signs).

If you are already familiar with the basics, you can skip this section, but if you read it anyway, you may discover something you didn't already know.

That's it. I hate long introductions. Enjoy the rest of the book.

PART I

INTRODUCTION

ASTROLOGY BASICS

WHAT THOSE STRANGE
SYMBOLS MEAN

KEY OF SYMBOLS

♈	Aries	☉	Sun
♉	Taurus	☽	Moon
♊	Gemini	☿	Mercury
♋	Cancer	♀	Venus
♌	Leo	♂	Mars
♍	Virgo	♃	Jupiter
♎	Libra	♄	Saturn
♏	Scorpio	♅	Uranus
♐	Sagittarius	♆	Neptune
♑	Capricorn	♇	Pluto
♒	Aquarius	⅂	Quincunx
♓	Pisces	ASC	Ascendant
'	Minutes of Arc	MC	Midheaven
⚶	Vesta	△	Trine
⚳	Ceres	□	Square
⚷	Chiron	✳	Sextile
⚵	Juno	℞	Retrograde
⚴	Pallas-Athena	☌	Conjunction
☊	Moon Node	☍	Opposition

UNDERSTANDING THE ASPECTS

Aspects are angles between planets. Well, why don't we just call them *angles*? Interesting story. Until a couple of centuries ago, astrologers didn't draw circular horoscopes; they made squares (Indian astrologers still do it that way). The Ascendant and Midheaven were at the corners of the square. Because of this, the Ascendant and Midheaven were called the "angles" of the horoscope. Since we call them the angles, we can't use the name angles for actual angles (go figure). So they came up with the term *aspects*.

In any event, ancient astrologers said that some aspects were *good* and others were *bad*. The *good* aspects were the trine (120°) and the sextile (60°). The *bad* ones were the square (90°) and the opposition (180°). The conjunction (0°) varied depending on which planets were involved. A conjunction between the "benefics," Venus and Jupiter, was considered good. A conjunction between the "malifics," Mars and Saturn, was considered bad. Today, we also use the 150-degree aspect. It's called the quincunx, and it can also be stressful.

Of course it's not really that simple. Today you'll see most astrologers use terms like easy and hard, or smooth and stressful. The reason is that sometimes the good aspects aren't so good and the bad ones aren't bad at all. Squares, for instance, can provide power. Sure they represent obstacles, but overcoming those will help you to grow.

I don't get too many clients who want their lives to be more difficult. Most people who come for a reading want things to be easier. That means sending them someplace where there are more sextiles and trines to the horoscope angles (Ascendant and Midheaven).

3

THE ASPECTS

Conjunction ☌
0° The *energies* of the two planets are merged together, for better or worse.

Sextile ⚹
60° A smooth, easygoing aspect. It makes things easier for us in an unobtrusive way, so we frequently take it for granted and don't pay it much attention.

Square □
90° We *always* notice the square. This is an obstacle that we have to overcome. Ancient books said terrible things about the square, but Toscanini had six of them in his chart and he did alright. (Ok, so maybe he murdered a few musicians; it was all for the sake of art). Squares are dynamic and give power.

Trine △
120° Trines tend to make things easier.

Opposition ☍
180° These are stressful because the planets are pulling against each other. We have to learn to find a balance point for each opposition.

Quincunx ⚻
150° This is a strange aspect. It can be on again-off again. Completing things is more difficult. When you think you have solved a problem, you find another problem (or challenge). There is less chance of a sense of completion.

THE PLANETS

The Sun ☉
The Sun is the heart of any horoscope.

The Moon ☽
The Moon makes things go up and down (like the tides).

Mercury ☿
Mercury is the planet of communications and transportation.

Venus ♀
Venus is the planet that makes things easier, makes them run more smoothly. If you get a flat tire when Venus is smiling on you, you will get it right in front of a service station.

Mars ♂
Mars is the planet of action and energy. It also rules arguments and fights.

Jupiter ♃
Jupiter is the planet of *good luck*, but you can have too much of a good thing. Jupiter also rules overconfidence and over-expansion.

Saturn ♄
Saturn is supposed to rule *bad luck*, but it does so much more. It can give discipline, persistence, and the ability to

plan long-range. It rules fear, but it also rules caution. Get your Saturn working right and you're home free.

Uranus ♅

Uranus is the rebel. When Uranus is around, expect the unexpected.

Neptune ♆

Neptune is the planet of dreams. It also rules illusion, delusion, and confusion.

Pluto ♇

Pluto is the planet of extremes. All or nothing. Life or death. The highest or the lowest.

Nodes of the Moon ☊

The *South Node* shows the place in life where we are comfortable. These are like our roots, but if we remain there too long, we get root rot. The *North Node* is the place where we eventually have to grow to, whether we want to or not. The South Node is always exactly opposite the North Node.

THE ASTEROIDS AND CHIRON

Don't worry too much about the asteroids. They are a minor influence. Concentrate on the planets first. Still, *anything* can have a strong influence if it is on the Ascendant or Midheaven, so check to see if Chiron or one of the asteroids is in close aspect to one of these angles. The asteroids can be useful for career if you happen to work in a profession that one of them rules. And how do you tell that? Take a look at the list.

Chiron ⚷

Chiron can increase your teaching ability. It can also make you more of a *maverick* than you normally would be. Try to keep it away from the chart Angles (Ascendant, Descendant, Nadir and Midheaven.)

Ceres ⚳

Ceres can be good in the 2nd house (money) or the 10th house (career) or the 6th house (daily work) if your work has to do with food, clothing, or agriculture. If you put Ceres close to the Ascendant or Midheaven, people will come to you to be *nurtured.*

Pallas/Athena ⚴

If you need to solve problems or recognize patterns, Pallas/Athena can help. If it is well aspected, put it in the 10th or 6th house to help with work and career issues.

Juno ⚵

Juno (unless afflicted) can enhance partnership. When it is in the first house and close to the Ascendant, Juno can give you the innocent look of a newborn baby. This could cause people to underestimate you. Depending on the circumstances, it could also cause them to not take you seriously.

Vesta ⚶

Vesta helps you focus in whatever house it happens to be in. It also shows what we have to stop doing in order to recharge. For example, if your birthday chart has Vesta in the 6th house (day-to-day work) you can't work 24/7. You will have to take an extra day off now and then to regain energy.

WHAT IS A BIRTHDAY HOROSCOPE?

What is a birthday horoscope and how is it different from a regular horoscope? The regular horoscope (your *birth chart*) is the one you were born with. You keep that chart for life and it never changes. Of course, the planets keep moving after your birth. Every year the Sun apparently returns to the same spot in the sky where it was when you were born. If you make a horoscope for the exact moment of the return (plus a minor correction), that chart is called a *Solar Return Chart*, or as I prefer to call it, the *Birthday Chart*. This one doesn't last for life. It will show a lot of the things that are going to happen to you during the coming year. Then it's over and you get a new birthday chart the following year.

But the nicest thing about the Birthday Chart is you can change it if you don't like it! All you have to do is be somewhere else on your birthday. You can give a twist to the wheel of fate by traveling to the right place at the right time. I've done it for myself and for thousands of clients. It works.

Like all horoscopes, the Birthday Chart depends on *where* you are as well as the time. Nobody can choose the location where they are born, but they can certainly choose where to be on their birthday. When you do that, you turn the horoscope wheel and change your destiny.

Astrologers have had different opinions about solar return travel for years. Some said that you had to set the birthday chart for the place of birth. Others said that you had to do it for the place of residence. Still others claimed that you could change the chart by being elsewhere, but that you had to stay in the new location for a whole year to make it work. To me, that last opinion made no sense at all. Some people are born on ships and airplanes. They literally move away from their birth location within minutes after being born, but the horoscope set up for that place is still their birth chart for life. The same thing should be true for birthday charts. You only have to be at the new location for a few minutes. After that, you should be able to move anywhere else and the chart will still be valid.

I had a chance to test this out in 1981. At that time I'd been practicing astrology for 10 years and was able to become a full-time astrologer right after my first birthday travel experiment. My birthday chart for New York was terrible. Pluto (planet of extremes) was afflicting the Moon and Sun. To make matters worse, they were all in strong sections of the horoscope (angular houses). In astrology, the Sun and Moon rule your body, and I certainly didn't want my body going to extremes. All I wanted to do was take these bad aspects and move them to weaker areas of the chart wheel. I also knew that the Sun gains strength if it is higher up in the horoscope. So where could I go to elevate the Sun and still have it in a weaker house? I tried a bunch of alternatives, and L.A. worked. I went there, stayed 36 hours, and came home.

Within 24 hours after I returned, my phone started to ring. And ring. And ring. All of a sudden, it seemed everyone wanted me to give them a reading. I took another look at the birthday chart. By accident I made the career and money areas strong. Very strong. I wasn't concentrating on career. All I wanted to do was reduce the effect of the bad aspects. My income more than doubled. It went from $9,000 to $19,000. That was the year I became a full-time astrologer. (Back in 1981, you could still live in New York on $19,000 a year. Those days are long gone.)

I've been traveling on my birthday ever since and spent it everywhere from Hawaii to Cairo. I have also sent clients all around the world. You'll see some of the actual cases here. But first, a *warning*.

CHAPTER
2

What Traveling on Your
Birthday Will NOT Do for You

Let's say that you're 97 years old and have to use a walker. If your dream is to qualify for the Olympics, I can tell you right now, no horoscope is going to help you. There is nothing short of a miracle that can make it happen. The same is true if you just dropped out of high school and you want to be a millionaire in the next two months. Your goal has to have a *reasonable chance* of being reached. That's the first caveat.

Second, you have to make some sort of *effort*. If you want a new job, for example, don't just take a birthday trip and then sit around and wait for someone to knock on your door and offer one to you. There was a story about a little old man who kept praying to win the lottery. "God," he said, "I've been good all my life. Please let me win the lottery." He kept saying the same prayer for years. Then one day, he heard a big, booming voice that said, "YOU'RE NOT DOING YOUR PART!" Right away, he knew that it was God speaking to him. "What do you mean I'm not doing my part? Haven't I been good all my life?"

"THAT WASN'T MY POINT," the voice replied. "YOU HAVE TO BUY A TICKET!"

Third, your *circumstances* have to be right. Another astrologer told this story. A woman came to her and complained that two other astrologers had told her she would meet the man of her dreams during the past year. It didn't happen. This astrologer looked at the chart and saw the same thing. Then she asked the woman to describe her typical day.

"Well," she began. "I'm a single mother. I work all day, come home and take care of the kids. By the time I get them in bed I'm exhausted, so I go right to sleep."

"There's your problem," the astrologer told her. "The only way you can meet Prince Charming is if he knocks on your bedroom door."

Circumstances can be wrong in other ways too. Let's say you want your business to increase, but the business you are in is manufacturing buggy whips, or 8-track recording tapes, or 45 rpm records. Forget about it. Those industries are dead.

So while the stars can push for you, if your circumstances aren't right, they will be pushing against a stone wall and nothing will happen.

Fourth, you have to remember that three-quarters of the Earth's surface is *water*. Sometimes the best place to be on your birthday is the middle of the ocean. Not easy to get to unless you have a yacht. Sometimes the best place is dangerous. The mountains of Afghanistan may be beautiful, but if you go there, they could be the last things you see. What do you do in a case like that? You go to the place that is *second* best, or even *third* best, and do the best you can for the next six months. On your next return chart, you will get another opportunity to improve your life.

Wait a minute. Did I say *six* months? Doesn't the birthday chart effect last a full year? Yes, but most of it happens in the first six months after your birthday. Six months later, the Sun will be opposite the place it was when you were born. If you make another horoscope for that exact time and place, that will be your *Half-Birthday Chart*. Yes, your half-birthday chart can also be changed by travel. So you get two chances a year to travel and improve your life.

Fifth, sometimes the planets just happen to afflict each other a lot. No matter where you go, there seem to be problems. In that case, you go to the place that is the *least bad*. That way, you can minimize the difficulties. At least the birthday chart can tell you what challenges you will be facing, and as the old saying goes, forewarned is forearmed. Brace yourself, take care of the problems, and six months later you will get another chance to travel and change your life for the better.

Sixth, sometimes the thing you want most is ruled by a planet that's *afflicted*. Let's say that you want to improve love and romance. Suppose on your next birthday, the planet Venus (which rules love and romance) is making a 90° angle (*a square*) with Saturn (difficulties and delays). No matter where you go, there will be problems. The same will be true if Saturn in your birthday chart makes a square aspect with your *natal* Venus (the place where Venus was when you were born). In these cases, you have to wait another six months and see what your half-birthday has to offer.

CHAPTER 3

WITHOUT THIS MINOR CORRECTION, YOUR BIRTHDAY CHART MAY NOT WORK SO WELL

The Earth moves around the Sun, but guess what? The Earth's *orbit* also moves around the Sun. That means the Sun has to (apparently) move a little bit extra every year in order to get back to the same place it was when you were born. And that little bit extra keeps growing year after year. Eventually, everyone's birthday winds up a day later. This correction has a name. It is called PRECESSION CORRECTION.

Back in 1990, I got a panicky call from a client. She said I made a "mistake" in her reading. Somebody pointed out to her that the degree of the Sun in her birthday chart was more than its degree placement in her birth chart. I told her that I always *precession-corrected* return charts. "I don't know what that means," she said. "All I know is that the numbers are different, so it must be wrong." I lost a good client over that; so now I tell all clients about "precession correction" at the start of their first reading.

There are two ways to do any return chart: precession corrected or not corrected. The experience I have had doing thousands of return charts since 1981 is that the precession-corrected charts *work*. I've also done comparisons with the non-corrected charts. Strangely enough, in many cases, the corrected and non-corrected charts can indicate the same things. But, whenever the charts show different outcomes, it is the precession-corrected charts that prove to be right.

Another astrologer, Celeste Teal, wrote *Identifying Planetary Triggers*. It is an excellent book with a lot of wonderful material on doing predictions. However, in the chapter titled "Introducing the Return," she writes:

Sufficient evidence suggests that the precessed chart patterns show events as they are experienced on a psychological level while the non-precessed chart patterns represent the way they are experienced on the material and earthly plane.

My experience (with several thousand charts and feedback from clients) is that exactly the opposite is the case. If you are interested in material results, the precession-corrected charts are the way to go. For evidence, read the case histories presented here in this book.

But how do you make a birthday chart? Even more important, how do you know where to go to change it?

PART II

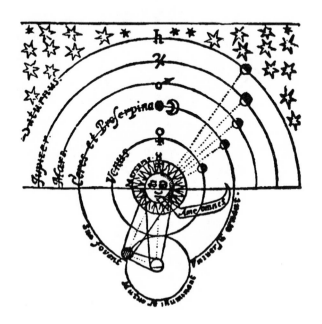

THE RULES

How do I Make a Birthday Chart?

You could try to do it by hand, but, before you do that, go to a psychiatrist and have your head examined. Only someone who is crazy or suffering from terminal masochism would calculate their own charts these days. The two best programs are *Winstar* from Matrix Software, and *Solar Fire* from Astrolabe (no, I am not getting a kickback for recommending them). There are others out there as well.

In addition, there are websites that will let you do return charts, but be careful. Some of them don't do *precession-corrected* return charts. How do you tell the difference? If the birthday chart (solar return chart) has the Sun in the *exact same position* as the Sun in your natal (birth) chart, then it is NOT precession corrected. In other words, if the birth chart has the Sun at 20° and 12' of a sign, and the return chart has it in the exact same place, then you have the wrong chart. In a precession-corrected chart, the Sun has to have a *higher number*. In the above example, the return Sun might be at 20° and 32'.

What's this thing about "minutes?" That's from the ancient Babylonians. They had a weird thing for the number 60. They were the ones that divided the circle into 360°. Then they decided to divide each degree into 60 parts, called minutes (represented by the symbol ').

Maybe one day, we'll use the decimal system, but not today.

Ok, so now you know how to make a precession-corrected birthday chart. Set one up for *your place of residence*. The next question is...

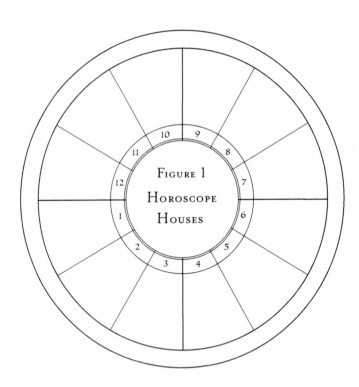

Figure 1

Horoscope

Houses

(decorative chapter icon)

What Part of My Life Do I Want to Improve?

Hey, that's up to you. You can change any area you like. Let's take a look. (**Figure 1,** horoscope houses.)

1ST HOUSE

This rules you. If you want to increase your energy and initiative, you may want to put Mars here. In 1983, I went to Milwaukee and put Jupiter (planet of good luck) right on the Ascendant. I was a bit luckier, but I also gained 11 pounds before I knew it. Couldn't fit into any of my pants. I forgot that the 1st house rules your outward appearance and that Jupiter makes things *expand*.

2ND HOUSE

Money! This house gets requested a lot. It covers more than money though. All material possessions are governed here. Beyond that, it also shows what you *value*. That includes the value you place on yourself. This is the house that shows your sense of self-worth.

3RD HOUSE

Communications, short trips, brothers, sisters, and neighbors. This is not a strong house and is generally a good place to put a planet that you want to weaken. If you have a lot of writing or communicating to do, however, put Jupiter, the Sun, or Mars here.

4TH HOUSE

Home, real estate. The parent of *lesser* influence. Usually, this is the father. If you're planning to buy or sell a home, this is the section of the horoscope on which to concentrate.

5TH HOUSE

Love and Romance! This house gets plenty of requests too. But it also rules children, gambling, speculation, sports, games, and *fun* in general. What most astrology books don't tell you is that the 5th house also rules *engagements*. If you want a serious relationship and are aiming for marriage, this is the house to work with.

6TH HOUSE

Your job and day-to-day work. Not career. That's the 10th house. The 6th house also shows relations with co-workers and subordinates. It also shows the outward *circumstances* of health.

7TH HOUSE

Marriage and partnerships. When I first started sending people traveling on their birthdays, I sent the ones who wanted marriage to places where their 7th houses were strong. The results were mediocre. Then it dawned on me that you have to meet them before you marry them! That means you have to make the 5th house strong because the 5th rules more than romance. It also rules *engagements*. If you live in a country where marriages are arranged, you can make the 7th house strong. In the United States and Europe though, you will do much better with the 5th house.

8TH HOUSE

Sex! And credit, credit rating, other people's money. You make this house stronger if you want one of these. Remember though, the 5th house rules romance. The 8th house only rules the physical act of sex itself. This house won't give you a relationship. If you already have a relationship and the sex is getting a little dull, this is the house to look to if you want to spice things up.

9TH HOUSE

Long journeys, higher education, publication, and "higher mind." In the horoscope wheel, the 9th house is opposite the 3rd house. Since the 3rd house rules short trips, the 9th rules long ones. The 3rd is writing, the 9th is publishing. The 3rd rules specific facts, and the 9th rules the synthesis of those facts into general principles. Hence, the 9th is the house of philosophy and *higher* education. Concentrate on strengthening this house if you are planning to enter a degree program or are about to take a long trip.

The 9th house also rules *legal matters*. I have had disagreements with other astrologers who say that lawsuits are governed by the 7th house. Not so. The 7th house rules *open enemies*, so it shows the person who is suing you (or whom you are suing). The legal matters themselves, however, are ruled by the 9th house. The bottom line is: don't put Saturn here if you are about to sue someone.

If you don't have any legal cases pending, this house is a good place to put planets like Saturn since the 9th is a *cadent* house. Planets placed here tend to be weaker.

10TH HOUSE

Career, public standing (your public image), and the goals of your life. The 10th house also rules your boss (authority figures in general), and the parent of greater influence (usually the mother).

11TH HOUSE

Traditionally, this house is said to rule friends, hopes, and wishes. It does more than that. The 11th house shows how you can deal with *groups* of people. This is the house to concentrate on if you want to expand your circle of friends, or if you have to do a lot of work with groups.

12TH HOUSE

Restrictions and places of restriction, such as hospitals and prisons. This is a good place to put a planet if you want it to be out of the way. *Warning!* If you are going to put a so-called *malefic* planet here (Mars, Saturn, Uranus, Neptune, or Pluto) make sure it's at least 6° away from the Ascendant and also, *make sure it's in a different sign from the Ascendant.* Why is this?

Years ago, another astrologer told me a story. It might have been an old legend, I don't know if it really happened. Supposedly, a few centuries ago, an astrologer was hired to choose a coronation time for a Holy Roman Emperor. It was a difficult job. No matter how he turned the wheel, something bad was going to happen somewhere (all astrologers get charts like this every now and then). Finally, he picked a time when Mars was going to be in the 12th house, 3° above the Ascendant and in the same sign. Three days after the coronation, the emperor was assassinated! After things calmed down, they hunted down the astrologer and had him beheaded. So if you are going to put a malefic planet in the 12th house, make sure it's in a different sign from the Ascendant and at least 6° away.

Why 6°? Because in a Solar Return Chart (and the Half-Solar Returns too), every degree is equal to one month. Each chart is good for six months, and then the next return chart takes over. Any aspect that is more than 6° from exact won't manifest until the chart has expired.

Is the 12th house good for anything? Yes. If you want to spend a lot of time in a religious retreat, this is the house to concentrate on. This house is also the one to work with if you are in intensive psychotherapy.

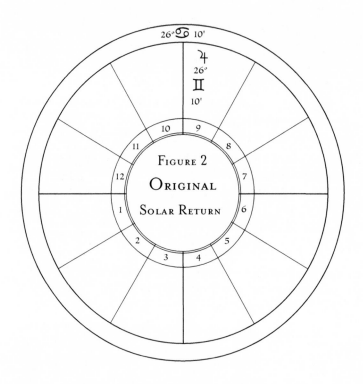

FIGURE 2
ORIGINAL
SOLAR RETURN

WHICH DIRECTION DO I GO?

It's best first to set up a birthday chart for your city of residence so that you will have a point of reference. Then, if you don't like the chart, you turn the wheel until you get something you do like. Let's take a look at a simplified example. Suppose you want to improve your career and your birthday chart (set up for your city of residence) looks like the one in **Figure 2**.

Jupiter, the planet of expansion and "good" luck is in house number 9. That's a weaker house which rules long journeys and legal matters. You want Jupiter to be in the 10th house, which rules career. In addition, you'd like to get Jupiter as close to the Midheaven as possible in order to magnify the effect. In order to do this, you have to turn the wheel *counterclockwise*. But which direction is that?

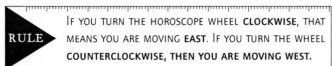

RULE — IF YOU TURN THE HOROSCOPE WHEEL **CLOCKWISE**, THAT MEANS YOU ARE MOVING **EAST**. IF YOU TURN THE WHEEL **COUNTERCLOCKWISE, THEN YOU ARE MOVING WEST.**

Ok, so you know from this example you have to move west. The next question is:

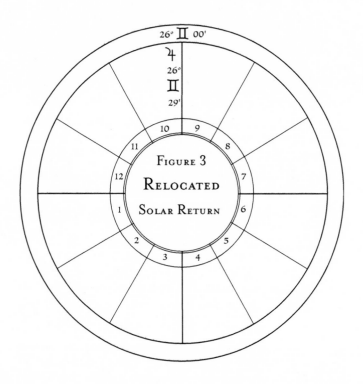

26° ♊ 00'

♃
26°
♊
29'

10 9
11   8
12 FIGURE 3 7
    RELOCATED
1   SOLAR RETURN 6
2   5
3 4

How Far Do I Have to Travel?

In the chart (**Figure 2**) Jupiter is 26° of Gemini and the Midheaven is 26° of Cancer. The signs of Cancer and Gemini are right next to each other. How big are signs? Signs are 30° each. First you have to go counterclockwise 4° to get from Gemini to Cancer. Then you have to go another 26° through Cancer to get to 26° of Cancer.

4° + 26° = 30°. You have to go 30° west from your place of residence to get Jupiter, planet of "good" luck in your career house.

Beginners sometimes make the mistake of *counting the houses* to figure the distance. Don't do it! Houses vary in size. Some are bigger. Some are smaller. Use the *signs*. They are all the same size (30° each).

Once you know the direction and how far to move, look at a map. Maps usually list the longitude degrees at the top and bottom. Find the longitude of the city where you live. In this example, you will have to add 30° to that number. Let's say you live in New York City. The longitude is 74° West. (West of what? West of Greenwich, England; that's the international standard.) 74° + 30° = 104° West. Look at your map again. Find 104°. Wait a minute. How can you do that? The map only has lines for 100 and 105°. No problem. Use the 105 degree line since that's the closest. 104° will be just a little bit to the right of that line.

Now look up and down that line. Do you see any cities? Yes. Denver is on the 104 degree line. So a trip to Denver will put Jupiter, planet of luck and expansion, on the top of your next birthday horoscope That is exactly what **Figure 3** shows.

CHAPTER 8

MORE RULES

So all I have to do is put Jupiter in the right part of the Birthday Chart?

NO!!! For one thing, Jupiter may be afflicted on that day. In that case, you will have to use another planet. More important though is what the other planets are doing. Suppose you want more love and romance. You put Jupiter in the 5th house (the house of love and romance), but the planet Saturn happens to land right on the Ascendant. That will make you feel like you're carrying around a big, heavy lead weight for the next six months. You'll be tired, depressed, and prone to illness. Not exactly the best situation for romance, is it? So here is another rule:

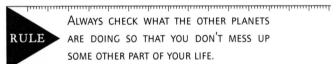

RULE ▶ ALWAYS CHECK WHAT THE OTHER PLANETS ARE DOING SO THAT YOU DON'T MESS UP SOME OTHER PART OF YOUR LIFE.

All right, I made sure that the other planets weren't making trouble in other parts of my life. Is that it?

Again, no. Now you have to check your *natal chart*, your birth horoscope, to make sure that there is no conflict with your birthday chart. I already mentioned that it's no good to have a planet like Saturn on the Ascendant in your birthday chart. But you will get the same bad effect if the Ascendant of your birthday chart is in the same degree as your birth Saturn (the place where Saturn was when you were born).

You have it easier here though. If the afflicting natal planet is more than one degree *behind* the birthday chart Ascendant, you're safe. That's because your natal planets *don't move* in relation to the planets in the return chart. The planets, Ascendant, and Midheaven of the return chart, however, *do move* forward at the rate of one degree per month. So all you have to do is make sure the Ascendant and/or Midheaven are at least *one degree past* any "malefic" planet (such as Saturn or Pluto). But more about that later.

PART III

HOW WELL DOES THIS WORK?

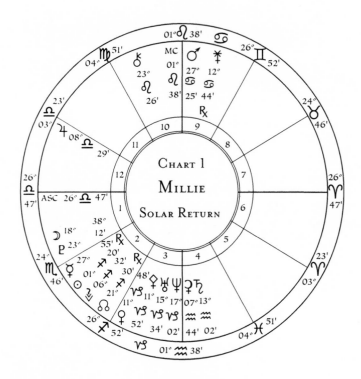

CASE HISTORIES

MILLIE, PART I

Her ex-father-in-law was rich, famous, powerful, and cheap. She was sure he was the one behind the tough time her ex-husband was giving her on the child support payments. Millie was also one of the most negative people I have ever met. She believed that disaster was around every corner. If she won the lottery, she would think the tax payments would send her to the poor house. Sometimes it is claimed that astrology can work through the "power of suggestion." The people who say this have never met Millie. Nothing could convince her that anything in the Universe was positive.

Mille had her hearing just before she came for the reading. The judge, she said, was horrible. He was nasty, sarcastic, and overruled every objection her lawyer had made. Was her legal situation going to improve? "Well," I told her, "not if you spend your next birthday in New York." **(Chart 1)** The sign of Gemini was on the cusp of the 9th house (legal matters) and Mercury, the ruler, was Retrograde. Even worse, the 7th house, which rules both marriage partners and open enemies (Not a coincidence!) had Aries on the cusp. Mars, ruler of Aries, was the highest planet in the chart (that makes it powerful) and it was in the 9th house (legal matters). If you want good luck, there is no substitute for Jupiter. Now how do you get Jupiter into the 9th house of legal matters?

NOTE: Some astrologers say that the 7th house rules legal matters. It doesn't. The 7th house rules open enemies. That includes people who sue you and people whom you sue. The legal issues themselves are shown by the 9th house. I have seen this again and again.

In New York, Jupiter is in the 12th house where it is out of the way and can't help much. To get it into the 9th house, you have to move it clockwise about 80 or 90°. Clockwise in a horoscope means *east*. Look on the map. Eighty to 90° east of New York puts you near Rome. Yes, Rome did put Jupiter in the 9th house. But I wanted to give Millie even more of a boost. Years ago, I read that if the North Node of the Moon is near the Ascendant, it increases your chances of overcoming enemies. I don't remember where I read this, but I had seen it work with two other clients. One had a lawsuit dropped right after he got back from his birthday trip. The other, within a month after her birthday trip, had a nasty neighbor suddenly move away.

Was it possible to get the North Node on the Ascendant of Millie's birthday chart while still keeping Jupiter in her legal house? Yes. The Midheaven is not affected much by moving north or south, but the Ascendant is. I looked on the map and saw that Copenhagen, Denmark, was directly north of Rome. Bingo! The Midheaven hardly changed, but the Ascendant moved clockwise to 22° of Sagittarius. The North Node was 21° of Sagittarius. Mission accomplished. Jupiter was still in the 9th house giving her luck in the legal area, and the North Node was right above the Ascendant **(Chart 2).**

When Millie came back from Denmark, there was another hearing with the same judge. He was now "very polite" (Millie's own words) and he ruled in her favor.

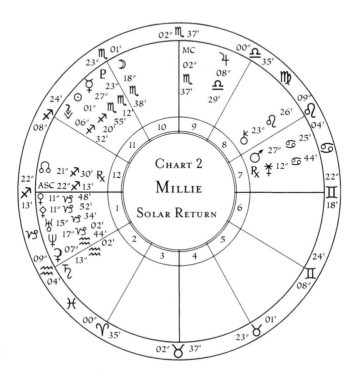

CHART 2
MILLIE
SOLAR RETURN

How can you possibly change other people by traveling on your birthday? You can't, but traveling does change *YOU*. Other people then react differently to those changes.

I didn't see Millie for a couple of years after that. She didn't travel on her half-birthday or her next birthday. Her ex-husband appealed, and six months later (when her Copenhagen chart was no longer valid) a higher court reversed the judge's ruling.

MILLIE, PART II

The next time she came to me, she was having job problems. She *hated* her job but she was afraid to quit. Make that too terrified to quit. More than "luck" with employment would be needed. Her courage would have to be bolstered.

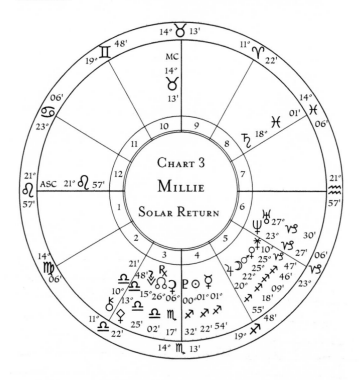

Millie's birthday chart for New York **(Chart 3)** had only one aspect to the Midheaven (career), and that was a sextile from Saturn. That was a good aspect, but Saturn increases caution. This would tend to keep her from moving ahead. Then I noticed that the planet Uranus was close to making a trine aspect to her Midheaven. All that had to be done was to turn the chart wheel about 12° clockwise. That means Millie had to be east of New York on her birthday. Antigua was the place.

The birthday chart for Antigua **(Chart 4)** put the planet Uranus (sudden change) right at the beginning of the 6th

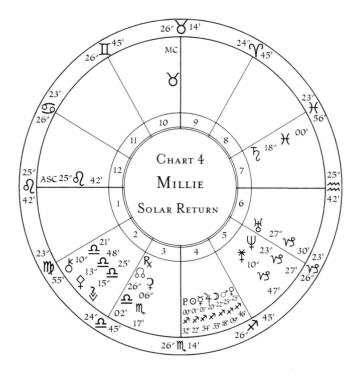

house (employment, day-to-day work) as well as giving it a trine (favorable) aspect to the Midheaven. When Millie came back from the trip, she walked right into her boss' office and quit. Could that could have been due to the power of suggestion? Yes, but what happened next could not. While Millie was cleaning out her desk, she got a phone call from someone who offered her a job with more money.

Remember that Uranus is the planet of sudden and unexpected events. It can turn your life into a roller coaster ride. A few days later, that new job fell through. But a couple of days after that, a better job offer turned up. This time it stuck.

Planets like Uranus and Pluto are unpredictable. If everything is going smoothly in your life and you want to keep it that way, avoid them. But if you have nothing to lose, then roll the dice.

SERINA

She was about to be "downsized." Her entire department was going to be eliminated. Was there someplace she could go on her birthday to increase the chance of getting a new job?

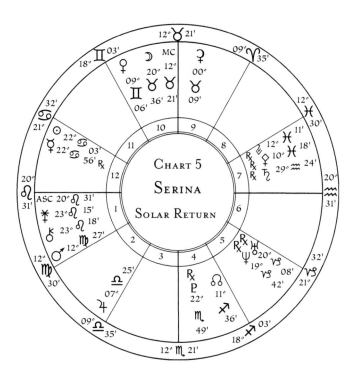

Her solar return for New York was a mess **(Chart 5)**. The Sun was in the 12th house. This can lower your stamina and make you feel restricted. Uranus was opposite the Sun and was also sitting very close to the cusp of the 6th house (work). If she stayed in New York, even if she could manage to get a new job, it probably wouldn't last too long.

Once you have the birthday chart for the place of residence, the next step is to look for planets making "good" aspects to each other, either a sextile (60°) or a trine (120°). There were plenty of those around in Serina's birthday horoscope. There is an opposition of the Sun-Mercury conjunction at one end and Uranus and Neptune at the other. There is another opposition between the Moon and Pluto. The bad effects of these oppositions are reduced because these planets also make "good" aspects with each other (trines and sextiles). This is the so-called "mystic rectangle" (draw lines to connect the planets and you get a rectangle), and it's supposed to be beneficial. Why is it called a "mystic" rectangle? Most likely because that sounds a lot better than just calling it a plain old rectangle.

If we put late Pisces at the top of the chart, we can get a lot of good aspects to the Midheaven. The Sun, Mercury, and Pluto would make trines, and the Moon, Uranus, and Neptune would make sextiles. We would have to turn the horoscope wheel about 48° counterclockwise, and that would mean she had to move west; 48° west of New York is San Francisco. This was a great chart, but, unfortunately, the Sun and Mercury didn't make it into the 2nd house (money), so I kept looking.

If I sent her east, Jupiter would be in the house of money *and* trine the top of the chart. The furthest east I could send her in North America was Saint John's, Newfoundland. Bingo!

What good is having luck in your career if you're not getting paid for it? It's not enough to make the career house strong. There has to be a connection with the money house (the 2nd house) as well. The Newfoundland chart did that twice over **(Chart 6)** First, Venus rules the sign on

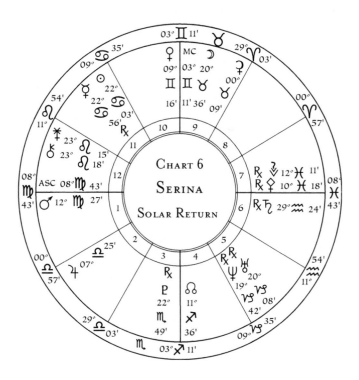

the money house (Libra) *and* Venus is in the 10th house (career). That's one connection. Jupiter, the planet of "good luck," was in the money house *and* it made a trine (a lucky aspect) to the Midheaven. That's a second connection. But Jupiter also has a trine aspect to Venus. That adds to the luck and makes another connection between houses 2 and 10 (career and money). That year, Saint John's Newfoundland was the place for Serina to be.

So what happened to her? A month and a half after her birthday, she called to tell me that her company did the downsizing and everyone in her department was terminated. Except her. She also got her old boss' office. The 10th house also rules the boss or any authority figure. Putting Venus up there meant that the higher-ups liked her and didn't want to let her go.

I had made the birthday chart *too lucky*, and she didn't need a new job after all.

ANONYMOUS

This client was terrified that anyone should discover their identity. I could only tell their story if I didn't mention anything personal about them, including their gender.

Anonymous owned a store in a building which the landlord was trying to vacate, and they were the last occupant. One cold December night, the pipes froze. When they thawed the next morning, the store was flooded and the stock was ruined. My client sued the landlord, and, as is usual in such cases, stopped paying rent (the rent money was put in an escrow account). The landlord saw an opportunity to evict them. He sued for non-payment of rent and aimed to get an eviction.

The courts in New York are jammed up with cases. It was going to take about two years for my client's lawsuit to get to trial. The landlord's suit was in *housing court*, which didn't have as much of a backlog. His suit was going to be heard first. My client's lawyer told them that they were in trouble. That's when they came to me.

How do you give someone "luck" with a lawsuit? The first thing that you do is give them luck with the judge. My client's birthday horoscope for New York City was terrible. Judges, bosses, and other authority figures are ruled by the 10th house, and that begins with the Midheaven. Take a look at that New York City chart **(Chart 7)**. The sign of Taurus is at the top. What rules Taurus? The planet Venus. And where is Venus? In house number 12, the house of hidden enemies. It's not exactly a good idea to make the judge your enemy.

Jupiter is the planet of good luck. What would it take to get Jupiter to the top of this horoscope? Count the degrees. In New York, 2° of Taurus is at the top. Jupiter is at 24° of Gemini. We have to move the Midheaven 28° to get to Gemini and then another 24° to get to Jupiter. That's a

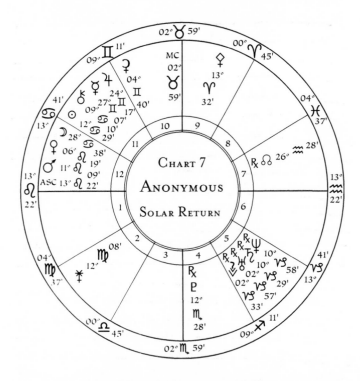

total of 52°. Which direction do we have to travel? Jupiter has to move clockwise to get to the top. That means you have to travel east. Now, what is 52° East of New York? Iceland! I sent my client to Reykjavík, Iceland **(Chart 8)**.

My client was one of those hysterical Cancers. They called me endlessly asking if I was sure. "All of my friends say that I am crazy," my client said. "Why are you telling everyone your business?" I asked. Their last call was late at night the day before the trip. Someone had told

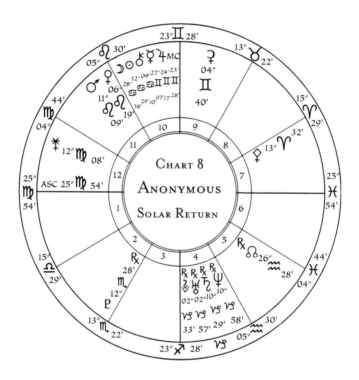

them that Iceland was a Communist country (this was in 1989, before the fall of the Soviet Union). "It's a member of NATO," I screamed. "Get out of here! Go!" After my client returned, I got a call saying, "I loved it! I'm going back there for a vacation."

What happened first? The judge who was trying the case seemed to be biased in my client's favor, but the luck didn't stop there. Six times, the landlord tried to serve my client with a summons. Six times he missed. My client called me each time to say, "He missed me again." Finally, the server gave the summons to the clerk in the store. The clerk was not an officer of the corporation. That was illegal. The judge threw the landlord's case out.

The landlord sued again. Once more, they couldn't find my client, even though my client was making no effort to hide. Again, they tried and missed six times. Once, they came in and served one of my client's customers. Another time, my client was in the store all day. Anonymous picked up the phone to make a call, but the line was dead. So my client went out to find a pay phone (this was in the days before cell phones). Guess when they came in to serve the summons? Right. When my client was out, of course. They missed again.

By this time, several months had passed. It was almost time for my client's half-birthday. Half-birthday horoscopes can either push in the same direction as the birthday chart and keep the momentum going, or they can slam on the brakes. They can even get things moving in the opposite direction.

The half-birthday chart for New York wasn't that bad. **(Chart 9)** Jupiter (good luck) was still in the 10th house (judges). But Jupiter wasn't in the same sign as the top of the chart. That weakened it. More serious was the fact that Venus ruled the 9th house (legal matters) and Venus was retrograde. Retrograde planets are weaker, and I didn't want any weakness in the legal area. Retrogrades also can *reverse* things, and that's the last thing you need when everything is going well. On top of that, Jupiter was making an opposition to Uranus. There is no place on Earth where you can send someone to change an angle between two planets. You have to go to a different part of the solar system, and the space shuttle doesn't do that yet. Fortunately, there is a trick that can deal with oppositions.

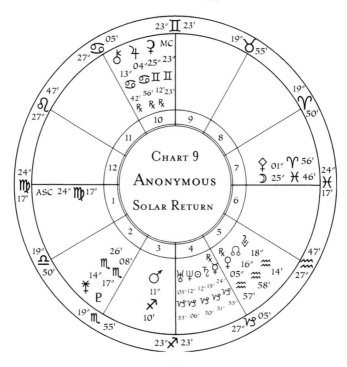

An opposition is 180° and is supposed to be a "bad" aspect. The "good" aspects are the sextile (60°) and the trine (120°). Guess what? 180 ° = 60° + 120° ! All you have to do is go someplace where either the Ascendant or Midheaven is making "good" aspects to both ends of the opposition. That way, you are taking something bad (the opposition) and having it do something good.

Use the Ascendant if you want to improve *relationships*. Use the Midheaven if you want to improve *business, career, or dealings with powerful people* (such as judges). I sent my client to London, England. Look at what that did to the Jupiter/Uranus opposition **(Chart 10).**

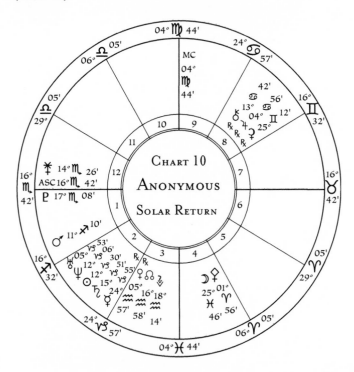

Uranus (sudden changes) is now in the house of money. When positive, that can bring a windfall. Jupiter rules the house of money (Sagittarius is on the house cusp). They are both making "good" aspects to the Midheaven, and the aspects are *applying* (forming) which makes them even stronger. Not only that, but the aspects are less than a degree from being exact. This makes them about as strong as you can get.

The legal house (house 9) has the sign of Cancer on the cusp. The Moon, ruler of Cancer, makes a "good" aspect (sextile) to Mercury. This aspect is also within one degree from being exact (again, powerful). Mercury rules the signs of Gemini and Virgo. Virgo is on the Midheaven (the judge) and Gemini is on the 8th house cusp (other people's money). What a chart!

The landlord caved in within a week after my client got back from England. He had to. My client was occupying the store, not paying rent, and couldn't be evicted. Not only that, but there was a multi-million dollar lawsuit for damages hanging over his head. He settled for $900,000 AND he forgave the one year of rent my client didn't pay. My client's attorney said, "Somebody up there must like you." My client told me, "I kept my mouth shut, but I was thinking, 'Yeah, Jupiter'."

RONY

Here is one client who gave me permission years ago to tell this one story on my television program. It happened nine years before I met him, so he was at the right birthday loca-

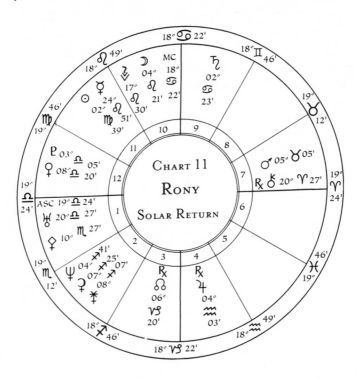

CHART 11

RONY

SOLAR RETURN

tion by accident. Rony became a major concert violinist, but in 1973, he was struggling and ready to give it all up. There was one more performance he had to give and then he would quit. The concert was in Manila, capital of the Philippines and, by coincidence, it was on his birthday. That meant his birthday chart would be set for Manila. In the audience was Imelda Marcos, the First Lady of the country.

She fancied herself a patroness of the arts, and she took him under her wing, introducing him to a bunch of big wheels in the classical music scene. Concert dates piled up. His career took off.

What was in that birthday horoscope **(Chart 11)?**

The first thing to do is check the *angles* (the Ascendant and Midheaven). Uranus is sitting within 2° of the Ascendant and square the Midheaven. Doesn't Uranus cause upheavals? Isn't it supposed to turn everything upside down? Well, it did, didn't it?

Now I don't recommend putting Uranus in a square aspect to the Midheaven if you are trying to improve your career because it can be too unpredictable. It's like a defibrillator. You use it in an emergency when the heart stops, but not when things are going well.

There was a lot more going on in Rony's birthday horoscope. The Moon is the ruler of his Midheaven, and it is in the 10th house (career). This makes it easier to get either yourself or what you do before the public. On top of that, the Moon is in Leo, sign of show business. That's very good for attracting attention. And just look at the aspects the Moon is making!

1. A sextile to Venus, planet of art (all of the arts). Venus happens to be in its own sign, and that makes it stronger.

2. A sextile to Pluto, the power planet, the planet of extremes. Pluto rules the sign of Scorpio. Where is Scorpio in this chart? On the cusp of house 2, the *money* house. This means the ruler of career (the Moon) is making a good aspect to the ruler of money. That's always a good thing to have if you want to get paid for your work.

3. A trine to Neptune, which is in the house of money. Neptune is one of the two planets that rule music (the other ruler is Venus). The career-ruling Moon is in good aspect to both. On top of that, Neptune is in the house of money. What sign does Neptune rule? Pisces. Where is Pisces in this chart? On the cusp of the 6th house, the house of day-to-day work. So the ruler of work is a music planet that's in the house of money, and it makes good aspects to the ruler of career and the ruler of the money house. Do you see a trend here? Career, money, work, and music are all connected *favorably*.

When it comes to luck, you have to look to Jupiter, and it's making good aspects all over the chart. It has a sextile to Neptune and a trine to Venus (the music planets), and a trine to Pluto (which rules the money house). Once again, we have a combination of "luck," money, music, and work.

The so-called "good" aspects will bring you luck, but they don't give power. If there are too many good aspects, you can just drift along expecting everything to go your way. Strange as it sounds, to get the most out of good aspects, you need some "bad" ones. And what better planet to give energy than Mars.

Mars has square aspects to both the Moon and Jupiter. One possibility is that there will be plenty of arguments caused by a short temper. But all of those good aspects shift the chart's direction to work, career, and money. Mars just provides the power.

Jupiter makes an opposition to the Moon. On the negative side, this can push you into taking on too much, biting off more than you can chew. Well that's what Rony did.

It was the luck provided by the good aspects that helped him to pull it off.

By the end of that year, Rony was able to buy a Stradivarius, and they are not cheap. He made it to

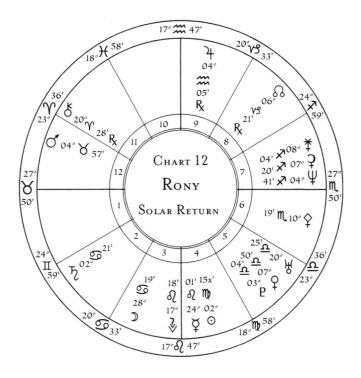

the top. One really good birthday chart made all the difference.

Now let's compare this with the birthday chart that was not precession corrected. The corrected chart had the Moon in Leo in the 10th house, and that is a perfect indicator of a powerful woman in one's life. The opposition from Jupiter and the sextile from Venus showed that this influence was going to be lucky for him. But where is the luck in the non-precession corrected chart, **(Chart 12)** the one that many astrologers still use? It's out of the way in the 9th house, where it doesn't have much influence on the career. Not only that, but Saturn (delays and obstacles) is in the money house. That is not a sudden jump in income.

Whenever the corrected and non-corrected charts differ, the precession-corrected charts win hands down.

LYNN

Lynn came to me in tears. She owned an apartment building that was half vacant. She was behind on the mortgage payments and the bank was threatening foreclosure. Her birthday chart for New York did nothing for her **(Chart 13)**. It didn't do anything bad, but it didn't do anything good either. The only aspect that affected business was a trine (120°, a "lucky" aspect) from Saturn to the Midheaven. Saturn is a planet that has its biggest effects when it's *afflicting* something. All the "good" aspects from Saturn do is produce a bit of stability.

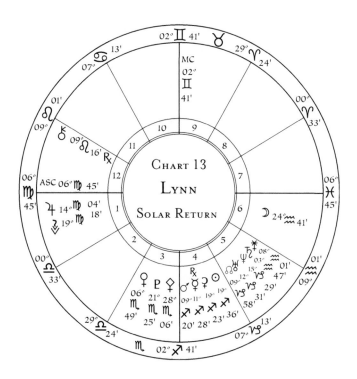

But Jupiter (good luck) was not too far from the money house (the 2nd house). If we could get it there, she would have a chance. Jupiter was at 14° of Virgo. If we could also get 14° of Taurus on the Midheaven (career), Jupiter would be making a trine. Check the other aspects Jupiter is forming. It has trines to Uranus (sudden, unexpected change) and Neptune (dreams and visions). They would also be making trines to the Midheaven. To get Taurus on the Midheaven, we have to turn the chart wheel counterclockwise. On the map, that means move *west* by about 18°: Des Moines, Iowa.

The birthday chart set for Des Moines **(Chart 14)** has Jupiter, Uranus, and Neptune forming a *grand trine* with the Midheaven. Now the Midheaven is not a planet. It is not even a physical body. It's only a point in space.

> **RULE** ▶ WHEN YOU HAVE TWO OR MORE PLANETS FORMING A GRAND TRINE WITH A CHART **ANGLE** (THE MIDHEAVEN OR ASCENDANT) AND THERE ARE NO PLANETS NEAR THE ANGLE, THE GRAND TRINE IS **NOT BALANCED** AND THE "ENERGY" OF THE PLANETS IS DRAWN TO THE ANGLE.

In this case, the "energy" of Jupiter (luck and expansion) Uranus (the unexpected) and Neptune (dreams and visions) was shooting into career and business. What were the results?

Lynn's birthday was in December. In March, she called me and said excitedly, "I can't talk to you right now," (only a Gemini or a Sagittarius will call to say that they can't talk to you!) "but the apartments are renting and I have somebody interested in renting the store. Bye."

By that May, the building was completely rented. In the meantime, her mortgage was sold to another bank. The new bank reduced her interest by a point and forgave over $2,000 in late fees that the other bank was charging. She also got a reduced assessment on her real estate taxes!

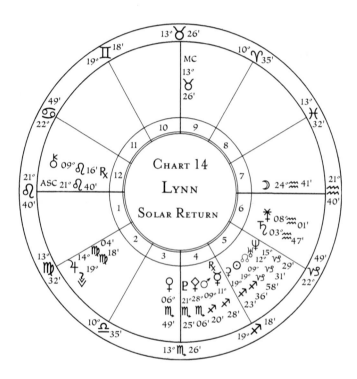

Now you might have noticed that going to Des Moines produced an affliction. Pluto, planet of extremes, made an exact square to the Ascendant. Why didn't that produce a disaster in relationships? It did just that with Arlene, whose case is on page 143. In Arlene's case, Saturn (bad luck) was afflicting too, and there weren't that many good aspects. With Lynn, there is the Grand Trine to the Midheaven, and that outweighs anything else in the chart. Still, you have to be careful. Keep the *angles* of the horoscope (the Ascendant and Midheaven) as free from affliction as possible.

EZEKIEL

You don't always need a lot of "good" aspects to get a great chart. A few well-placed planets with the right connections can easily do the job. Zeke was the kind of guy whose enthusiasm was always getting him into trouble. He is a real estate agent who always trusted his bosses (big mistake) and never liked budgets (big mistake number two).

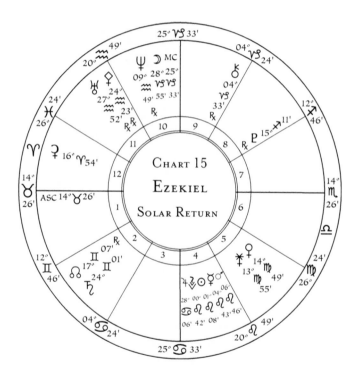

When Zeke came to see me, he was already in debt. His New York City birthday chart **(Chart 15)** had Saturn, the "bad luck" planet in the money house. I've seen a case where the person actually made a lot of money when that happened, but he said he was putting in overtime every night. Usually, Saturn there means extra difficulties, so it's not exactly the planet to use if you're having money problems.

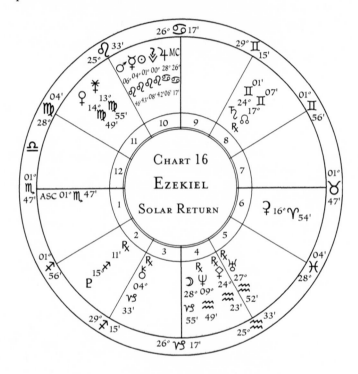

There was an opposition aspect between the Moon and Jupiter. If it weren't for that 2nd house Saturn, the New York chart wouldn't have been so bad, because both the Moon and Jupiter aspected the Midheaven. But what good is luck in career if you don't make money?

A good move to make when there is an opposition is to go someplace where both ends of the opposition make "good" aspects to the Midheaven. The New York chart has the Moon right on the Midheaven, so we would have to turn the horoscope wheel either 60° or 120°.

Sixty degrees west of New York is Juneau, Alaska. No good. The house of money is weak there. No planets are in it, and the ruler of the sign on the cusp is Neptune. Only one aspect to Neptune, and that's an opposition from Mars. Money would flow out as fast as it came in. That assumes any money would come in at all since Neptune (when afflicted) indicates deception. Zeke had already been ripped off enough. Scratch Alaska for this birthday.

If the wheel is turned 60° to the East instead, Zeke would wind up in the Canary Islands. Still no good. Now Mars is in the 2nd house (money) and it is still opposite Neptune. There are no decent aspects to either planet, so there would still be money troubles.

The next thing to try is turning the wheel 120°; 120° east of New York is Baghdad. Forget it! 120° west of New York is the Pacific Ocean. No islands are nearby. Zeke would have to be in the water.

So what's left? The only other alternative is to put Jupiter right at the top of the birthday horoscope. In New York, Jupiter is at the bottom. That means you have to turn the wheel upside down. To do that, we have to send him to the other side of the world. Jakarta, Indonesia **(Chart 16)**.

Putting any planet at the top will strengthen it. Jupiter ("good" luck) is in the sign of Cancer, and that makes it pretty strong to begin with (Jupiter is "exalted" in Cancer). So we have the planet of good luck in the house of career, but what about money? The sign on the cusp of the 2nd house, house of money, is Sagittarius. That's the sign ruled by Jupiter. The planet of good luck (Jupiter) rules the money house and is in the career house. That's a strong connection between money and career. Jakarta, Indonesia was the place to be.

Business picked up for Ezekiel within a week after he returned. His commissions increased over 50% from the previous year.

KIMBERLY, PART I

The first time Kimberly came to me, she wanted fame and fortune. Her birthday chart for New York wasn't bad **(Chart 17)**. The sign of Leo was at the beginning (on the cusp) of the house of money (house 2). The ruler of Leo (the Sun)

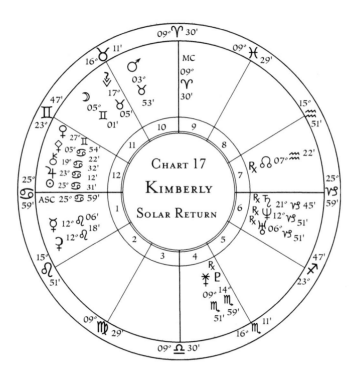

was right next to Jupiter (good luck). But they were both in the 12th house (hidden things) and that made them weaker. Why not make them stronger? After all, you can't do better than a Sun/Jupiter combination. Now how far would we have to send her to put the Sun and Jupiter in the 2nd house (money)? And in which direction?

We have to move the Sun and Jupiter *counterclockwise.* That means we have to send her to the *west.* How about Chicago? The Sun and Jupiter would be making trine

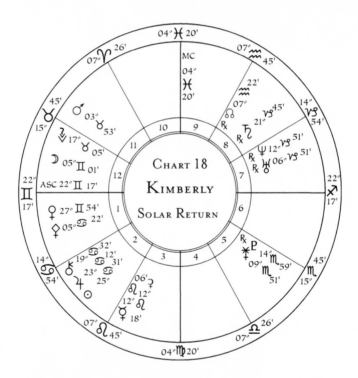

aspects to the Midheaven. No, not good enough. They wouldn't be in the house of money. How about Dallas, Texas? Yes, that puts them in the money house. But now, the Moon rules the Ascendant (Cancer) and the Moon is in the 12th house (restrictions). When the Ascendant ruler is in the 12th house, you feel, well, restricted. It's worse in this case because the Moon is also *intercepted.* It's in a sign that does not appear on the cusp of any house. That restricts her Moon even more. Who wants six months of feeling miserable?

El Paso Texas gets rid of the interception **(Chart 18)**. It also changes the Ascendant sign to Gemini, so the Moon is no longer the Ascendant ruler. The Midheaven (career and life goals) has good aspects (sextiles) from Mars and Uranus. Since Mars is *action* and Uranus is the *unexpected*, that should get her career moving. Notice that the Midheaven is also on the midpoint of Mars and Uranus. That means fast action. Yes, it can also mean *accidents*, but since both of these planets are making good aspects, that wouldn't be likely.

Right after she returned from her birthday trip, Kimberly got on the quiz show *You Bet Your Life*, hosted by Bill Cosby. She won several thousand dollars.

KIMBERLY, PART II

A year and a half later, Kimberly wanted something different. "Could you send me someplace on my Half-Birthday?" she asked. "My love life is dead." What do you do if you want something to *expand*? The rule here is:

> **RULE** — When you want something expanded, use Jupiter.

Kimberly's birthday chart for New York had six planets in the house of work **(Chart 19)**. Not exactly what she was asking for. She actually did have the sign of Sagittarius at the beginning (cusp) of her house of Romance (house number 5) and that sign is ruled by Jupiter. But look where Jupiter is. It's located in the previous house. Bad news.

> **RULE** — No matter what house you are looking at, the previous house always represents its **RESTRICTION** and **UNDOING**. If you're trying to improve romance, it makes no sense to restrict it.

Let's try to get Jupiter into Kimberly's romance house. But first, we have to check and see if Jupiter is forming any "afflicting" aspects. Nope. Jupiter has only one aspect, and that is a trine (120°; a favorable aspect) to the Moon. Okay, we can use it.

Since Jupiter is in the 4th house, we have to move it counter-clockwise to get it into the 5th. That means west.

Denver, which is about 31° west of New York, should do the job **(Chart 20).** Going to Denver also took those six planets in the work house and put them in the partnership house. That should bring even more people into her life. Little did I know how well that would work.

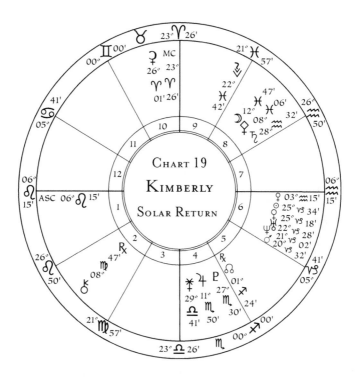

Those six planets would also make a favorable sextile aspect (60°) with the Midheaven. I thought this would improve Kimberly's career as well. What I forgot is that the Midheaven also shows one's *public* image.

A short time after her trip to Denver, Kimberly came back for an update. Her first words as she came through my front door were, "No more guys!"

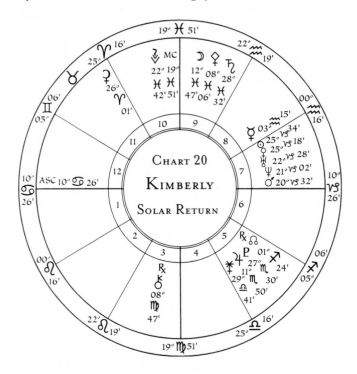

"What happened?" I asked. Oh, things picked up all right. One of her friends got Kimberly on a TV talk show. The topic for the day was "Women Who Couldn't Find Dates." Since it was a national show, she got calls and letters from all over the country. Right after I gave her that update, the show was re-broadcast. The Post Office started to deliver her mail in boxes. She also had to have her phone number changed.

For the next four or five years, every time Kimberly came for her update she would ask where to go to improve money and career. What happened here is a good illustration of the old saying: Be careful what you wish for, because you can get it.

CARRIE

A psychic once told Carrie that she would die "across the water and far from home," so she was quite upset when I told her to go to Barbados. "Are you sure I'm not going to die?" she asked. The problem (for me) is she kept asking it

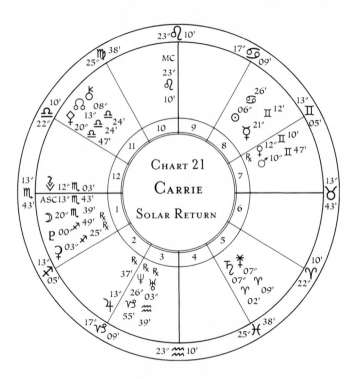

again and again, calling me almost every day for several weeks.

Carrie's birthday chart for New York was OK but not great **(Chart 21)**. Sure Jupiter ruled the sign (Sagittarius) at the beginning of her money house, but there was no connection to the Midheaven (career). And yes, Jupiter was also in the money house, but it was at the very end. That made it weaker.

The Barbados chart, on the other hand, had Jupiter much earlier in the money house **(Chart 22).** On top of that, Jupiter was now the chart ruler because its sign (Sagittarius) was on the Ascendant. If money is what

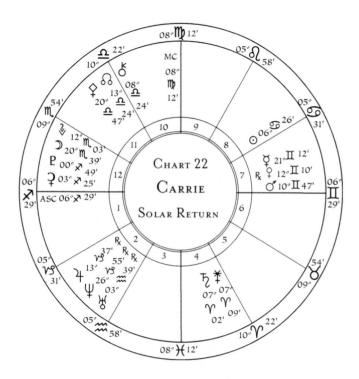

you want, it usually helps to put the Ascendant ruler in the money house. Jupiter also now made a trine to the Midheaven. The aspect was wide, but still within the limits.

Why didn't I send Carrie further to the east to make that lucky aspect stronger? In the Caribbean, the only thing further east than Barbados is water. If you look at the map, Newfoundland is further to the east, but it is also a lot further north. The sign Jupiter was in (Capricorn) would have been "intercepted." Planets in intercepted signs are weaker.

In the birthday chart for Barbados, the Sun (a lucky influence) was in house 8. That house rules "other people's money and possessions." Carrie was in real estate. Her whole business was dealing with other people's possessions. The Sun also made a favorable aspect (a sextile) to her Midheaven. Yes, Mars and Venus made square aspects to the Midheaven as well, and squares are "stressful." Remember though, that we need a stress aspect to activate the good ones. The square from Venus wouldn't count for much here. All that does is make you lazy and self-indulgent. That, however, would be taken care of by the extra energy from that Mars square! On top of that, there would also be a trine from Saturn to the Ascendant. That increases ambition and discipline.

The night before Carrie left for Barbados, she left a message on my answering machine. "I told all my friends that you said I wouldn't die on this trip. If I do die, they're going to spread the story all over town and ruin your reputation!"

About six weeks later, I bumped into Carrie on the street. "How have things been since you got back?" I asked. "The month after I got back, I made over $8,000 in commissions," she replied. "That's more than I ever made in one month before." She had a really sour look on her face as she said this. It was almost like she was disappointed that something good happened.

A couple of years later, I bumped into Carrie again. "I feel terrible," she wailed. "I'm so upset. I went to another astrologer and he told me I was going to die in two years or four years."

"What!" I yelled. "How dare he say something like that. That's so unprofessional! What could have ever possessed him to say such a thing?"

"I asked him," Carrie said.

Some people just like to suffer.

JAMES

James wanted to be a writer. More than that, he wanted to be a *published* writer. And he wanted to be a *well-known* writer. This means we would have to make two houses strong. The 10th house is career and public image, and that is a must for dealing with career. The 9th house rules *publication*. He needed a boost there as well.

His half-birthday chart for New York had Saturn (difficulties and obstacles) close to the chart bottom **(Chart 23)**. That meant it made an opposition aspect to the top of the horoscope. The top of the chart (the Midheaven) is career and public image. Obviously, that's not the best thing to have unless you think your life is too easy and you like to suffer. What made it worse was the square aspect that Mars (arguments) was making with both Saturn and the Midheaven. The 9th house of publications was ruled by Saturn. That would focus the difficulties (and possible arguments) on publication and publishers. Obviously, James had to travel.

Do we put Jupiter at the top again? No. Why not? Because Jupiter expands your *primary* career first. James was a lawyer. If we put Jupiter at the top, he might be flooded with cases and have no time to write. If writing is your goal, look to Mercury.

In the New York chart, the Midheaven is 8° of Aquarius. Mercury is 26° of Scorpio. I've done so many of these relocations, I've learned to do them in my head. Every sign is 30°. If we move Mercury 2 signs closer to the Midheaven, that's 60° and lands us at 26° of Capricorn. 4° more gets us to the next sign, Aquarius. 8° more gets us to the Midheaven. That's a total of 72° counterclockwise. On the horoscope wheel, counterclockwise is *West*.

New York City is 74° west of Greenwich. 74 plus 72 is 146. Now look at the map and find what is around 146° west of Greenwich. That puts James right in the middle of the Pacific Ocean. Fortunately, there are islands there, like Tahiti.

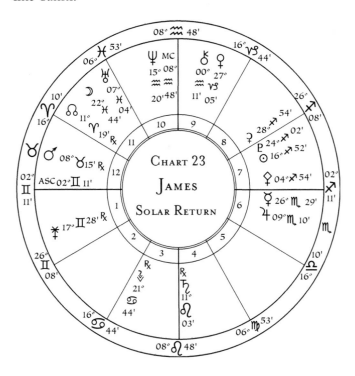

What does the Tahiti chart do **(Chart 24)**? First of all, Mercury makes a conjunction to the top (the Midheaven, the career). The Moon is forming a good aspect (a trine) to Mercury, and now it is also making a trine to the Midheaven. That makes it easier to get

85

your name before the public. Venus (the arts) makes a sextile to the top. Mercury at the top also means that people will be talking about you. The good aspects from the Moon and Venus mean what they say will tend to be favorable.

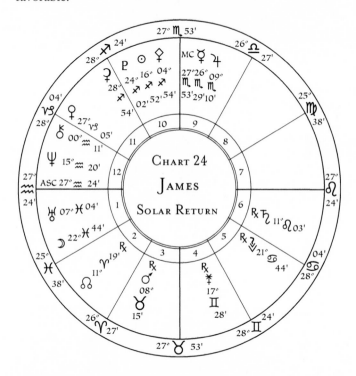

CHART 24

JAMES

SOLAR RETURN

What about Jupiter ("good" luck)? It's now in the 9th house, the house of *publications*. The Tahiti chart did it all.

So what happened? It rained the entire time James was in Tahiti. He wound up spending the whole trip in his hotel room writing. That got him off to a good start. When he got back, a publisher called to ask if he would translate a book from Russian to English (James speaks Russian fluently). He had also written over 300 pages of his own original material, but he was too busy writing to look for a publisher during the following few months.

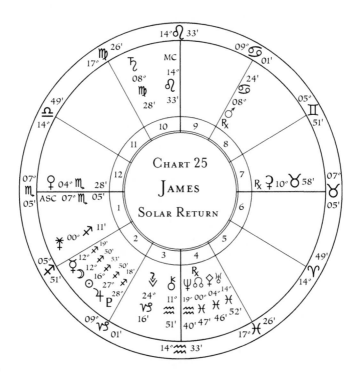

His half-birthday chart wasn't that bad for New York, but Venus was in the 12th house **(Chart 25)**. If I sent him west to get Venus into the 1st house, he would have lost that big, beautiful trine of Mercury (writing) to the Midheaven (career). I sent him to Ottawa, Ontario, Canada **(Chart 26)**. That kept the Midheaven pretty much in the same place, but the Ascendant moved back enough to place Venus in the 1st house.

There was an unexpected side effect from this. Women started to approach him. He didn't have to initiate contact. He now has two girlfriends (a Gemini Sun Sign prefers more than one of everything). He has a little less time for writing now, but he isn't complaining.

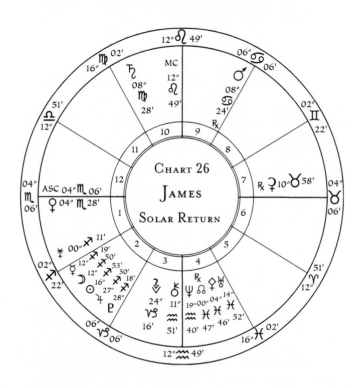

ME

Everyone talks about their successes because it makes them look good. But failures can teach us a lot too. Here is one of mine. A big one.

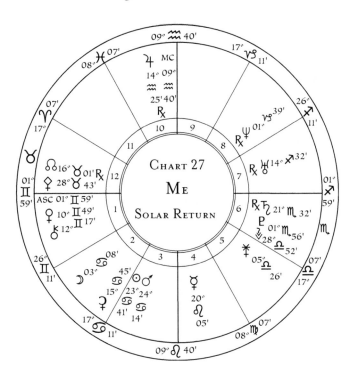

In 1985, I traveled to Cincinnati on my half-birthday to improve my career **(Chart 27).** Venus (love) was opposite Uranus (the unexpected). Take a look at the half-birthday chart and see where this combination landed. Venus was in the first house (me), which increases charm, while Uranus was in the seventh house (sudden change in partnership).

I met her the night the return was exact!

She was already engaged to someone else. Her fiancé had wanted to take a trip to Arizona a few months earlier. Coincidently, that was at the time of her birthday. Her solar return for Arizona put Uranus, that's right, in her house of marriage, right on her Descendant.

The bottom line was that she broke her engagement, sold her business, moved to New York, and married me, all within three months.

We both were very much in love and told all of our friends that when we met it was like being struck by lightning. That should have been the first clue (but it never is). Lightning only flashes for a brief instant, and then it is gone. Of course, like all things electrical, lightning is ruled by Uranus.

After we had been married three months, we literally woke up one morning, looked at each other, and said, "What did we do?" I had chosen a good day for the wedding, so we had a very friendly divorce.

 RULE — What the planet Uranus brings together suddenly can break apart just as suddenly.

WHAT CAN HAPPEN IF YOU ARE IN THE WRONG PLACE: THE CASE OF O.L.

His Lunar return was the worst chart I had ever seen **(Chart 28)**. Yes, lunar return charts also have an effect, although not *normally* as much as the solar and half-solar charts. Sometimes a monthly chart can have a really powerful effect, as it did here. In O.L.'s lunar return, Mars and Mercury were making an *exact* conjunction. By itself, this could have merely meant arguments, or perhaps

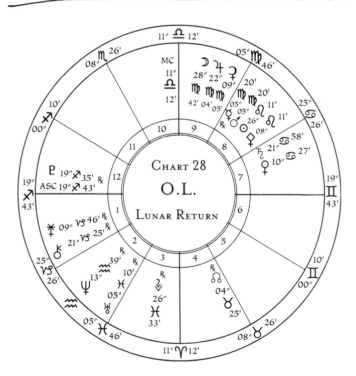

CHART 28

O.L.

LUNAR RETURN

a lot of energy going into communications. But Mars and Mercury weren't alone. Uranus was opposite both of them, and the angle was less than one degree from exact. Stress aspects between Mars and Uranus are accident prone. Mercury rules transportation. But the worst part was Pluto a fraction of a degree above the Ascendant.

Remember the story I told you earlier about the Holy Roman Emperor who was assassinated? NEVER put a malefic planet right above the Ascendant.

I told O.L. to travel west to get the Pluto out of the danger zone. Even then, I said, he might still have an accident (since the Mercury, Mars, and Uranus afflictions were so strong), but at least the danger would be minimized. He told me he couldn't travel because he was in a play.

What could I do? I told him to avoid driving unless absolutely necessary, and that if he did drive, to be very careful. On September 10 at 3:30 in the morning, someone cut him off on the West Side Highway in Manhattan. He lost control of the car, went into the oncoming lane, and rolled over. Another car in the oncoming lane hit him head on. O.L. was killed instantly.

ANA

Ana was going for a PhD and her 2003 birthday chart had Neptune, which can cause confusion, in the 9th house (higher education) AND it was making an

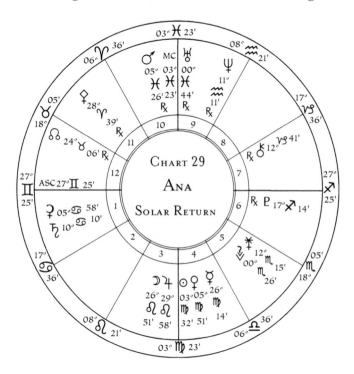

afflicting aspect (150°, known as the *quincunx*) to Saturn (more difficulties). Ana was also having problems with faculty members. The top of the chart (the Midheaven) rules bosses and authority figures. Look at what's in **Chart 29**. Mars, planet of arguments. I HAD to get her out of New York!

Mars was opposite both the Sun and Venus. One of my favorite moves is to turn the horoscope wheel so that both ends of an opposition will make "good" aspects to the top of the chart. For Ana, that meant moving her 60° either east or west. 60° west of New York is Juneau, Alaska. 60° east are the Canary Islands.

The birthday chart for Juneau had Aries on the Ascendant. Mars, the ruler of Aries, was in the 12th house (restrictions, psychological problems). No, Juneau was not the right place.

Now take a look at the chart for the Canary Islands **(Chart 30)**. Five planets made good aspects to the Midheaven. That did it. These are the results in her own words:

TRAVELING ON MY BIRTHDAY

One Friday night in 2003, while channel surfing cable TV, I came across a rather formal-looking man talking about astrology. In addition to giving some fascinating explanations of famous peoples' charts, he was talking about an odd concept: traveling on your birthday and half-birthday to influence the important events for those times. I began tuning in to the show every week. Traveling on your birthday seemed crazy to me, but I made an appointment to see Bob Marks anyway. I expected to be amused. I expected to think it was silly. But at the end of that first 3-hour reading, I went straight to a bookstore, bought travel books for the Canary Islands, a large map of my destination, La Palma, and booked air tickets to be there on my birthday.

Let me explain my life situation and my pressing problem at the time of that first reading. I urgently needed to finish my doctoral dissertation, I'd been stuck for years, and time was running out. When I met Bob, I was 58

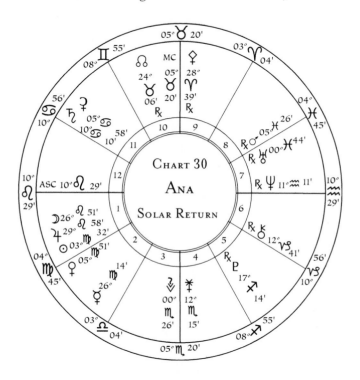

years old, with no job, taking Prozac by the handful, and trying to craft a new research design with very little support from my school department. The clock was ticking and the bills were mounting. Bob decided that the Canary Islands looked to be the best place for my solar return, so I purchased a ticket and off I went.

From there, it was like dominos falling over, one after the other. As I continued, seemingly insurmountable obstacles were met and conquered.

The next week in research seminar, as I explained my research design yet again, the same professor who'd kept telling me it wouldn't do, said, "Well, that seems fine. Go ahead with it."

When I had to learn SPSS, a statistical software program, two Chinese students I barely knew took me by the hand and gently showed me the rudiments of it.

I almost hired an expensive, unreliable research design consultant, but a freak airplane accident intervened. I ended up with a much nicer, hand-holding woman, who cost one-third of his price.

An Institutional Review Board application had to be approved for my research. There were problems with the application, but lo and behold, a new professor in my department also served on the review board. She interpreted the board's queries, helped me fix my application, and it was approved.

Finally, my dissertation was finished and ready for the hearing which would determine whether it was accepted or not and whether or not I'd be addressed as "doctor." Three days before the hearing, I flew to San Francisco and back in 31 hours, to improve some aspects in a lunar-return chart so that people would respond favorably to what I said.

Usually these hearings are characterized by tough questions to the candidate. Two of my classmates whose hearings took place the same week, came out of their session in tears. But the committee said my dissertation was one of the best they'd seen in years. The chairman said it was the best-written dissertation he'd *ever seen*.

I traveled to emphasize academic success for at least two more trips. I wrote a paper on my research. Others in the field had predicted I'd never get it published because I was an unknown, single author, but its submission was requested for a special issue of an international journal. It was published in 2006. I was asked to present the paper in a conference with top names in the field. The second paper is almost complete, and it too has been requested for publication by the editor of a prestigious journal. Last spring I was on television representing the organization which was the subject of my research. This fall, I'm co-presenter of a workshop on the topic, and this time, they're paying me to do it.

WRONG PLACE, PART II: THE CASE OF ARLENE

I had just given a lecture on traveling on your birthday at the *National Council for Geocosmic Research* winter conference in New York. She came up to me and asked if I could take a look at the horoscope for her last birthday. "Everything has been *horrible* since then," she said. Every now and then an astrologer sees a chart that makes them feel nauseous. This was one of those.

Remember *Rule Number One* is to keep the Angles (the Ascendant and Midheaven) free from affliction. Remember, too, that major aspects that are less than one degree from exact can have a *powerful* effect. Take a look at Arlene's birthday chart **(Chart 31)**. Pluto is less than half a degree away from an exact square to the Ascendant. The aspect is *forming*, which makes it even stronger.

The Ascendant and Descendant should be considered as a unit, as the Ascendant-Descendant axis. Aspects to this axis affect how we start things (Ascendant) and relationships (Descendant). This is the marriage and partnership axis, but it also shows how we deal with all one-on-one relationships.

Within eight hours after the chart went into effect, Arlene had a major argument with her fiancé, and he "stormed out," never to return. Pluto rules all sorts of volcanic eruptions. That was just the beginning. About two months later, her doctor was arrested for a major insurance fraud. Guess what he did to get a lighter sentence? He accused some of his patients of being in cahoots with him. Yes, he accused Arlene.

The F.B.I. paid her a visit and threatened her with jail. It cost $55,000 for a tax attorney and a forensic accountant to prove she never got any money from her doctor's fraud.

What he did was to have his patients sign blank insurance forms. Then, he filled in whatever informa-

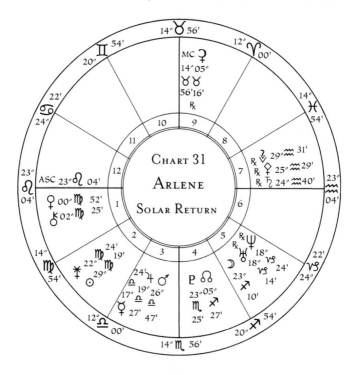

tion he wanted to later. He did $600 worth of work for Arlene. On the form, he said it was over $60,000. Later, he told the F.B.I. that he kicked back $9,000 to her.

Because of the work of the tax attorney and the forensic accountant, the government dropped the case against

Arlene. However, Blue Cross sued her and she settled with them for $12,000. "Why did you settle?" I asked. "You didn't do anything wrong." "I just wanted my life back," she replied.

Consider Arlene's case a warning. Keep the *angles* of the chart (the Ascendant and Midheaven) free from affliction. But aren't some afflictions "good"? Don't they activate the chart? Yes, but only when you have a greater number of "good" aspects (sextiles, trines, and favorable conjunctions) to those same angles. Even then, try to keep stress aspects from being too close to exact. Get them at the least more than one degree away from exact (any aspect within one degree from exact is powerful).

Another point: if you have to have a stress aspect, see if you can make it *separating* instead of *forming*. If an aspect is separating, it is weaker. Now how do you tell if it is separating? Let's look at an example.

You have to remember that the Ascendant and Midheaven move faster than any planet. It can take a planet a whole day to move a degree. It takes the Ascendant and Midheaven about 4'! Let's say that you have a birthday chart where the Midheaven is in Aries 20° and 15'. Suppose Mars is in Capricorn, 18° and 27'. In order for the aspect to become exact, Mars will have to move up to 20°. But the Midheaven moves *faster*, so Mars will never catch it. The aspect is *separating*. In other words, it already happened and now is past.

Suppose we had Mars at 20° and the Midheaven at 18°? In that case, the Midheaven would have to catch up to the Mars. No problem. The Midheaven moves much faster. The aspect is *forming*. In other words, it hasn't formed yet. It is in the process of becoming exact.

The point is, you may be able to tolerate a stressful aspect if it is separating. If you have a good aspect, it is better if it is stronger. In that case, go to a location where it will be forming. And do it fast.

What does the Non-Precession Corrected chart show? Take a look at **Chart 32**. Where are the prob-

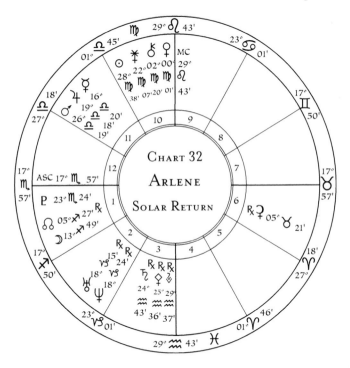

lems with partners and underhanded enemies? There aren't any! In fact, the Ascendant-Descendant axis has favorable aspects from Uranus and Neptune. Whenever the precession-corrected and non-precession-corrected charts show different outcomes, the precession corrected charts will show what actually happens.

MIA

Mia had been a member of the Yugoslav National ski team a dozen years earlier. Now she was living in New York and needed a job. Her birthday chart for New York **(Chart 33)** had Jupiter (luck) and Uranus (the unexpected) in the

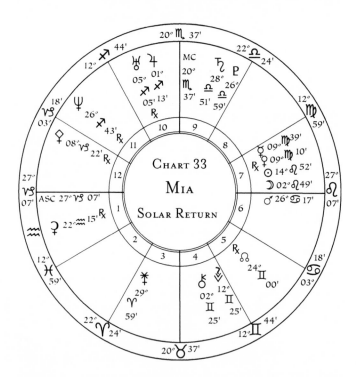

10th house (career), but they were not in the same sign as the Midheaven. That weakens the effect. To get them at the top, I had to turn the horoscope clockwise. That meant sending her *east* at least 10°. Ten degrees east of New York is the Atlantic Ocean. She would have to go

north to Canada or South to the Caribbean. Barbados put both planets right at the top **(Chart 34)**.

Why not put Jupiter exactly on the top? After all, it is the planet of "good" luck. The Midheaven in Barbados is on the Jupiter/Uranus *midpoint*, and it is still conjunct both planets. That gives you more bang for your buck.

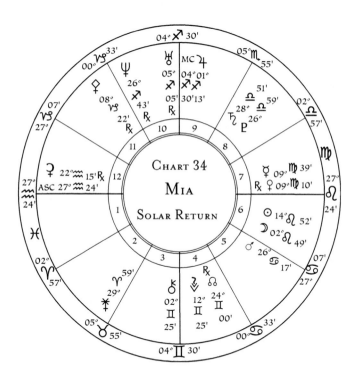

During the reading, I also told Mia that she could be successful in television. After she returned from Barbados, she applied for jobs at the major networks. When she went to ABC, *by accident* she wound up in the wrong office (Uranus rules all sorts of accidents, and not all accidents are bad). They were looking for people to help cover the 1984 Winter Olympics in Yugoslavia (it was still one country back then). Mia told me she normally wouldn't have applied for the job because there were several thousand applicants. But since she was right there anyway, she applied. Yes, she got the job.

If the job you're applying for is a long shot, a conjunction from Uranus can actually help, especially if Jupiter is close by. Don't use conjunctions of Uranus in normal circumstances.

WRONG PLACE, PART III: THE CASE OF DIANE

Diane said she absolutely couldn't travel on her birthday. Her birthday chart made me gag **(Chart 35)**. It was the first time I wished I had an airline sickness bag when I wasn't on an airplane. Saturn was opposing the Moon. OK, you can't change angles between planets, but take a look at where they are in the chart. Saturn was right at the top and the Moon at the bottom. Remember, Rule Number One is:

 RULE KEEP THE ANGLES FREE FROM AFFLICTION!

So what happened to Diane?

A month after her birthday, there was a knock on her door. It was a law officer who informed her that she was about to be evicted immediately. "That's impossible," she told him. "I paid my rent. I've got the receipts." It turned out, though, that her landlord had not paid the mortgage. The bank now owned the house and they wanted her out, pronto.

Diane got a new place to stay, but no lease. Unfortunately (it's amazing how often a chart with a strong, afflicted Saturn leads us to say "unfortunately") her new landlord happened to be dating the best friend of Diane's ex-husband. God only knows what he said, but the new landlord also wanted Diane out, pronto. She had to move in with a guy who had an alcohol problem.

Now what house does Saturn rule in the birthday chart? Saturn rules the sign of Capricorn and Capricorn is at the beginning (cusp) of the 3rd house (transportation). A passing police car noticed that Diane didn't renew her sticker on the windshield. They seized her car. She now had to pay the sticker and a fine on top of that or the State would sell her car. The problem was she spent all of

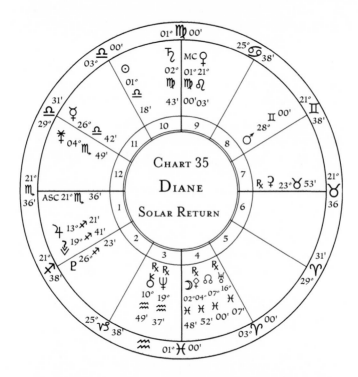

CHART 35

DIANE

SOLAR RETURN

her money moving. Somehow, she has to survive until her half-birthday when the chart will be better.

Okay, the first eviction would have happened anyway. Saturn (bad luck) was opposite the Moon (home). But traveling a bit east, at least to Tucson, would have weakened the affliction.

Maybe she could have avoided the second eviction. Maybe the police wouldn't have noticed her sticker had expired (she never paid the sticker fee on time and had never been caught before). We'll never know. All we can say is what did happen, and it wasn't good.

Once again, the Rule is:

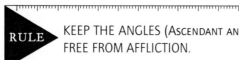

RULE ▶ KEEP THE ANGLES (ASCENDANT AND MIDHEAVEN) FREE FROM AFFLICTION.

WRONG PLACE, PART IV: THE CASE OF GWEN

This is another case of a very strong monthly return chart (the Lunar return). I didn't see this one until after the fact. Take a look at **Chart 36.** When I saw this chart, I wanted

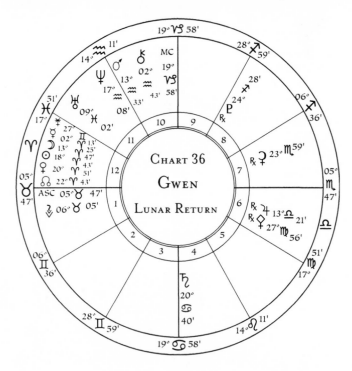

to spray it with garlic and drive a stake through its heart. Look at the large number of planets in the 12th house. That's the house of restriction and self-undoing, the house that rules both prisons and hospitals. Take a closer look. The Sun and Moon are both there and there is about to be a *Solar Eclipse*. How can you tell that? The Moon is approaching the Sun and both are near the Moon's North Node. Eclipses, of course, are raw power.

The Ascendant is ruled by Venus, and Venus is also in the 12th house. The Ascendant ruler is the ruler of the horoscope. Wait, we're just getting started. Remember to keep the Angles of the horoscope (the Ascendant, Descendant, Midheaven, and Nadir) free from affliction? Look at the bottom of the chart. Saturn is there *exactly*. On top of that, Saturn is making another stress aspect (a square) to the Sun and Venus.

There are only two possibilities here. One is that she will make someone in power angry (Saturn opposite the Midheaven) and wind up in jail (12th house). The other is that she will be going to the hospital (also the 12th house). A few days after the return, Gwen fell down some stairs (Saturn rules falls) and broke her left knee (Saturn rules Capricorn, sign of the knees). She had an operation and then went to a nursing home for a few days to recover. They gave her the wrong medication, there were complications, and she had to stay for six weeks. Saturn is also the planet of bad luck and delays.

So once again, check all of your return charts and keep the angles free from affliction.

LORRAINE

Lorraine's natal horoscope screamed "show business" and reeked with talent. Her biggest desire was to direct, but she was stuck in a dull office job that she was afraid to leave. Her next major return chart was her

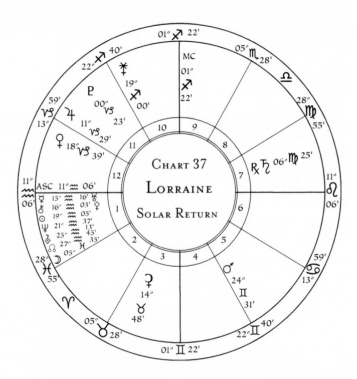

half-birthday. The chart for New York didn't do much **(Chart 37).** The last degree of Pisces was on the cusp of the 2nd house (money), and that's a degree that can cause trouble. The Fixed Star "Scheat" is there, and it has a Saturn-like influence. On top of that, both the Moon and Saturn were making stressful square aspects to the

Midheaven (career). That could mean increased instability and difficulties. However, if we turned the horoscope wheel counterclockwise, we could get both Venus and Jupiter to make sextiles to the Midheaven. She would have to be about 15° further west of New York. That's New Orleans **(Chart 38).**

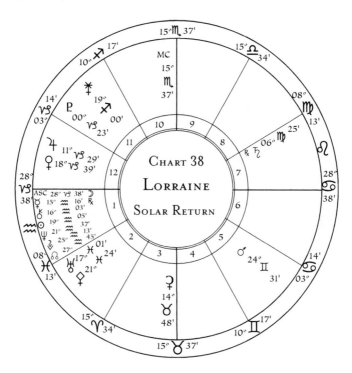

CHART 38
LORRAINE
SOLAR RETURN

The New Orleans chart also put Uranus (sudden changes) in the house of money, AND it made a trine to the Midheaven. That's my favorite move. Put a planet in the money house and make it trine the Midheaven. That way, money and career are both strengthened, and they feed into one another. The Midheaven is also aspecting the Jupiter/Uranus midpoint (sudden luck). The Sun and Mercury square the Midheaven, but you always need a square or two to provide energy. Squares from the Sun and Mercury are mild and shouldn't hurt.

After Loraine returned, she started searching for the show business jobs she really wanted. She was offered a director's position in a regional theatre. Yes, she accepted.

JOE

Joe works on Wall Street and the market was starting to be shaky. His next return chart was his half-birthday. If he stayed in New York, Saturn would be in the 1st house

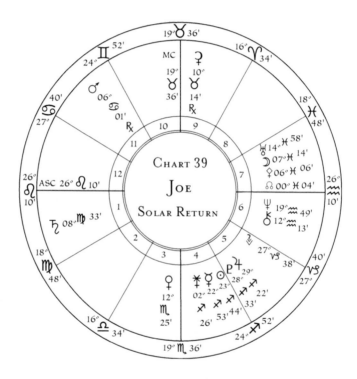

(Chart 39). What does that do? Let's put it this way. Did you ever feel like you were carrying a big, heavy *lead weight* day and night? Saturn in the 1st house can make you feel tired and depressed. But I noticed Venus made trines with the Moon and Uranus. Could we send Joe someplace so that they would all trine the Midheaven? I'd have to send him *east*, and the only thing east of New York is the

Atlantic Ocean. Fortunately, the ocean has islands. And one of them is Iceland. Iceland in December? Well, the chart was great, and hey, at least it wouldn't be during their busy season **(Chart 40).**

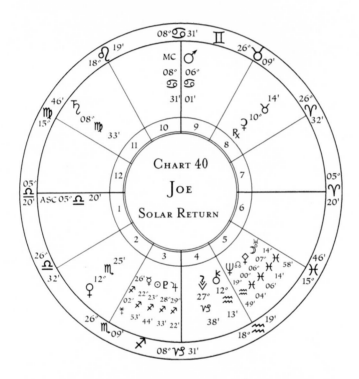

Venus is in the 2nd house (money) and it rules the sign on the cusp (beginning) of the house. It's not as strong as Jupiter, but it is still "lucky." Venus is forming trines to the Moon and Uranus. In the Iceland chart, the Moon rules the Midheaven (career), and Uranus rules the house of speculation (which includes the stock market). So we have the ruler of career, the ruler of speculation, the ruler of money, and the Midheaven all making favorable trine aspects to one another. And the Sun, Jupiter, and Pluto all make lucky sextile aspects to the cusp of the money house. Can you say Grand Slam? The energy is provided by Mars, which is conjunct the Midheaven.

Joe got a much bigger year-end bonus than he was expecting. It was over 25% larger than his best previous year.

One Last Thing

There you have it. You've seen the rules and how they work in actual cases. Some charts can be relocated easily. Others take more time and effort. Getting the right location for your birthday horoscope is only the first part. After that you have to take the trip!

People sometimes tell me they don't like the place I recommend for their birthday trip, and ask me if I can send them to someplace that's more fun. I always ask if they ever tell their doctor, "I know the medicine you're giving me will make me all better, but I don't like the taste. Can you prescribe chocolate cake instead?"

Remember it's nice to go to a place that you like, but the real reason to travel is to make your life better once you get back. So Happy Birthday, Bon Voyage, and Good Luck!

APPENDIX

What the Planets Mean in Return Charts

Planets in return charts mean pretty much the same as they do in your birth chart. The main difference is that they will have an influence only for the length of time the return chart is in effect.

THE FIRST HOUSE AND ITS PLANETS

The 1st house rules you and how you start things. It's an *angular* house, and that means any planet placed here gains in strength.

The Sun
The Sun in the 1st house is a good placement to have if you want to get noticed on a personal level.

The Moon
The Moon in the 1st house means you should watch your mood swings.

Mercury
Mercury in the 1st house is great for communications, but you'll probably talk a lot more than you normally do.

Venus

Venus in the 1st house increases charm, attractiveness, and makes social relations easier. The downside is it can make you lazy. Personally, I never cared about that. In fact, I enjoyed it.

Mars

Mars in the 1st house increases energy and desire for action. Watch out, though, for a tendency to argue. Actually, it's the people around you who should watch out... for YOU.

Jupiter

I put Jupiter in the 1st house for my 1983 birthday. In fact, I put it right on the Ascendant within one degree. After all, it is the planet of "good luck" and this is one of the strongest points in the horoscope. Unfortunately, I forgot that the Ascendant also rules your personal appearance. I gained 12 pounds before I knew it. Couldn't fit into any of my pants. You CAN have too much of a good thing.

Saturn

Saturn in the 1st house can make you tired and depressed. Saturn in the 1st house will make you feel like you are carrying a big, heavy lead weight. If you must put Saturn here, please make sure that it is as far away from the Ascendant as possible, and preferably in a *different sign* than the Ascendant. That will weaken the effects.

Uranus

Well, things won't be dull. Uranus in the 1st house is an accident-prone placement. Again, make sure that Uranus is towards the end of the house, as far away from the Ascendant as possible, and preferably in the next sign.

Neptune

Neptune in the 1st house is good for the imagination, but you may be a bit absent-minded. There's a lot more to say about the meaning of Neptune in the first house, but I forgot.

Pluto

Pluto in the 1st house makes you stronger and more intense, sometimes to the point of obsession. You may not notice it because the *energy* gets projected outward. But the people around you will notice. If you are the kind of person who wants things to stay as they are, you may feel under pressure with this placement. The best way to deal with that is to *throw things out*. Pluto is the planet of *elimination*. Getting rid of things helps to drain off the planet's "energy."

The Nodes

The *North Node* is like a little Jupiter. It protects you but, unlike Jupiter in the 1st house, it won't make you fat. The ancient interpretation is that "your enemies will dissolve before you." The first time I saw the North Node in the 1st house in a birthday chart, the client told me that they didn't have any enemies. Shortly after their birthday trip, they called to tell me of a terrible neighbor they had forgotten about, someone they had taken to court. Less than two months after my client's birthday, the neighbor suddenly moved.

In another case, the day my client returned from their birthday trip, they were notified that a lawsuit against them had been dropped. No reason was given.

The *South Node* in the 1st house can drain you, especially if it is close to the Ascendant. It can also give you a temporary feeling of inferiority.

THE SECOND HOUSE AND ITS PLANETS

The 2nd house shows your money and possessions. It also shows your values, including the value you place on yourself. The 2nd house shows your sense of self-worth. If you want to advance in your career, be sure to make this house strong too. After all, what good is a great career if you don't get paid for it?

The Sun

The Sun in the 2nd house is a positive influence and tends to increase money and possessions. Since the 2nd house also rules your *sense of self-worth*, this placement can make you feel good (or at least better) about yourself.

The Moon

Ups and downs. Be careful about putting the Moon in the 2nd house unless it is well aspected. Money comes and GOES more than it normally does.

Mercury

Mercury in the 2nd house is a good placement if you make your money through communications or transportation. If well aspected, it helps you with communications and negotiations concerning money and goods. If poorly aspected, you will tend to talk your way out of good deals.

Venus

In the 2nd house, as always, Venus makes things *easier*. When well aspected, it brings cash (of course, if Venus is in Virgo, it may be in pennies). When poorly aspected, you can waste your money and resources through laziness and indifference. You can find yourself saying, "I don't know what happened. I left the house with $100 and it's all gone now. It just seemed to disappear."

Mars

The plus side of Mars in the 2nd house is you will have the impetus, the *get-up-and-go*, to make money. Remember: Mars is *action*. Money can also go out fast if Mars has some stress aspects. Be especially careful if Mars makes a conjunction, square, or opposition to Neptune. That can cause you to lose money through confusion (the things you buy look good, but really aren't) or outright deception.

Jupiter

My personal favorite! I always try to put Jupiter in the 2nd house and have it trine (120° from) the Midheaven. Jupiter tends to *increase* things, and this is the house of money and possessions. A trine to the Midheaven gives a boost to career as well. Check out the stories of people who had Jupiter in the 2nd house to see the actual results. It works best if Jupiter is also well aspected by other planets.

Remember, if Jupiter is *afflicted* (has some stress aspects and no favorable ones) *DON'T* put it here. Under those circumstances, Jupiter will increase your money *outflow* and you'll be broke before you know it.

Saturn

No, Saturn in the 2nd house of your birthday chart does not mean you're going to lose all your money. I had a client who came to me the first time a few months after his birthday. There was Saturn in the 2nd house. "Money troubles lately?" I asked him. "No," he said. He was making money hand over fist. "I bet you're working hard though," I said. "Are you kidding?" he responded. "I'm putting in overtime every night."

You can make money with Saturn in the 2nd house, but be prepared to work extra hard. This placement can also mean a delay in payment. That might not be much of a problem for a Monthly Chart. You would just get paid the following month. With a birthday chart though, you might have to wait six months to a year (in other words, until the next cycle or half-cycle).

Uranus

Uranus in the 2nd house is good if you get your money from hi-tech, anything electronic, very new or strange.

126

It's also good if you happen to be self-employed or are in sales and get paid on commission. Oh yes. It's also good to have if you are an astrologer. If Uranus makes "afflicting" aspects, watch out for sudden financial losses.

Neptune

Neptune in the 2nd house is a good placement if you earn a living from any profession ruled by Neptune. That includes being a musician (or anything having to do with music, including production work) photographer, video production, or anything connected with art. On the scientific side, Neptune rules the profession of oceanographer and marine biologist. Neptune rules the sign of Pisces, a sympathetic sign that has an urge to take care of the poor and sick. This includes the professions of social worker and therapist.

If Neptune has stress aspects, be careful of your money and possessions. You could lose them through confusion or deception.

Pluto

Pluto in the 2nd house is a good placement to have if you are broke. Pluto rules "death and rebirth," so if your money is dead, this can increase the chance that it will make a comeback.

The Nodes

The North Node acts like a little Jupiter ("good" luck) and is good for bringing money to you. Remember, that the 2nd house is about more than money. It rules your *values*. The North Node in the 2nd house is good for pursuing what you value most, whatever that may be.

The South Node in the 2nd house means that finances can take on tremendous importance and can override every other consideration.

THE THIRD HOUSE AND ITS PLANETS

The 3rd house rules communications, short trips, brothers and sisters, neighbors, and your immediate neighborhood. This is a *Cadent* house, which means it is weaker. Therefore, this is usually a good place to put *difficult* planets, like Saturn, or planets that have too many *afflictions*. Don't do that if you are having trouble with a sibling or a neighbor, because that could make it worse.

The Sun

A positive influence (unless afflicted). The Sun in the 3rd house helps with communications and short journeys. This is a good placement if you want to improve relationships with siblings or neighbors. It is not that good if you want to get noticed; writers are the only exception.

The Moon

The Moon in the 3rd house gives you an emotional need to talk. If it's afflicted, you'll reveal too much to the wrong people. If it is well aspected, your communications can reach people on an emotional level.

Mercury

Mercury rules Gemini, the 3rd sign. That means Mercury will also be strong if it's in the 3rd house. This placement makes it easier to communicate, especially if you have to do a lot of writing or speaking, but you may find yourself talking too much.

Venus

Venus in the 3rd house makes things easier. Unless it is afflicted, it will make your communications more charming. It will also make for smoother relations with siblings and neighbors.

Mars

Mars in the 3rd house is a great placement to have if you want to tell someone off. If you're a writer working on a deadline, this is a godsend. Starting to write won't be a problem. Stopping might. If afflicted, be careful of arguments, especially with siblings and neighbors. If Mars is afflicted by Uranus, be careful of accidents during *short* journeys.

Jupiter

Jupiter expands things wherever it goes. In the 3rd house, it expands your mind and speech. If it is afflicted, be careful of making promises that you cannot keep. Since Jupiter is so optimistic, it can make you think you can do things that you really cannot do. This influence works both ways. An afflicted Jupiter in the 3rd house can also make other people more likely to over-promise things to you. Another minor drawback of Jupiter in the 3rd house is no one will believe you if you tell them you're depressed because your communications will *seem* so optimistic and cheerful.

Saturn

The 3rd house is one of my favorite places to put Saturn. It's out of the way here and is less likely to cause trouble. However, *don't* put Saturn here if your goal is to have better relations with your brothers, sisters, or neighbors. You'll be fighting an uphill battle. Also, do not put Saturn here if you are planning to buy a new car. Remember that the 3rd house rules transportation and Saturn rules *Murphy's Law*: If something can go wrong, it will go wrong, when you least expect it and at the worst possible time.

Uranus

Ok, if Uranus is in the 3rd house you're going to say some shocking things. It makes life interesting. This is a good position for learning something new, especially if it's *unusual, strange,* or even a little *shocking.*

Neptune

Neptune in the 3rd house is great if you're a poet, novelist, or a Hollywood screenwriter. For the rest of us, communications can be more vague and confusing, especially with siblings and neighbors. You may also find yourself getting lost on short trips more than you normally do. Generally though, it's nothing too serious.

Pluto

There used to be a TV commercial for a brokerage firm that went, "When E.F. Hutton talks, people listen." That's Pluto in the 3rd house. Your words will seem to have a greater than normal impact on those around you. This is great if you happen to be in advertising or sales. It's a great placement for psychologists and therapists too, because your words can literally heal, but they can also kill. Be careful of arguments because your words will be magnified out of all proportion.

The Nodes
The North Node in the 3rd house means you must concentrate more on specific day-to-day details (3rd house) and less on big-picture abstractions (9th house, where the South Node is).

The South Node in the 3rd house means the opposite. Day-to-day details can bog you down. You're more likely to be working on the wrong things and going in the wrong direction because you are not getting the big picture. The South Node in the 3rd house can also take every little thing personally and make mountains out of molehills (thanks to Patricia Konigsberg for that one).

THE FOURTH HOUSE AND ITS PLANETS
The 4th house shows *the end of the matter.* In a return birthday chart, it shows the end of your year. It also shows your home and your base of operations. This is the house to concentrate on if you want to buy or sell a home or do any real estate transactions.

The Sun
The Sun in the 4th house should make you happy (sunny) at home. The Sun is a lucky influence, so this is a good placement if you want to do real estate transactions. But *please* make sure that the Sun doesn't have afflicting

aspects. If you also want to improve your career, put the Sun close to the beginning of the house. Doing this will make the Sun oppose the Midheaven, ruler of career. The opposition of the Sun to the Midheaven is *not* bad. The beginning of the 4th house is called the *Nadir* and is one of the strong points of the chart. A conjunction to the Nadir will increase the strength of any planet.

The Moon

The Moon in the 4th house isn't bad since this section of the chart rules *home*, and the Moon is the natural ruler of home. You will tend to be more emotionally attracted to your home for the next six months and will probably spend more time rearranging things.

Mercury

Mercury in the 4th house could give you an urge to move since Mercury is a restless planet. By itself though, it's not enough to make you take the plunge. You will probably find yourself reading, writing, and especially talking around the house more than you normally do.

Venus

Venus in the 4th house is a good placement if you want to pretty up your house. If you are living with others, Venus here makes those relationships smoother. This is also the place to put Venus if you are planning to throw some parties in your home. And yes, it does make real estate transactions go easier. If you are buying or selling a home, Venus in the 4th house of your birthday chart is a plus.

Mars

If you have Mars in the 4th house, watch out for arguments in the home, but you can avoid them if you keep busy. Mars is, after all, the planet of action. But if things slow down, Mars gets bored and creates a "diversion." This is a good placement to have if you want to get personally involved doing some heavy, physical work at home.

Jupiter

Jupiter is the planet of good luck and expansion. If the Jupiter is afflicted in the 4th house, you could bite off much more than you can chew, or you will just feel so good, you won't get anything done. On the positive side, Jupiter in the 4th house can give you luck with real estate transactions. Even if you have good aspects to Jupiter, be careful that you don't overextend yourself. Since the 4th house rules *the end of the matter*, you could have a burst of good luck at the end of the chart's time period, just before your next return chart.

Saturn

There are three possibilities with Saturn in the 4th house: (1) you are depressed around the house, (2) you are very busy around the house, or (3) you are so busy outside the house that you have no chance to go home. Make sure the first one doesn't happen. Don't buy a new home if Saturn is in your birthday chart's 4th house. Be elsewhere on your birthday and get the Saturn out of there. If you aren't buying a home, you may still have trouble with your house. This Saturn placement increases the chance that things will break down and need to be replaced.

Uranus

Avoid putting Uranus too close to the beginning (cusp) of the 4th house. This is the planet of *sudden and unexpected change*, and when it is at a strong point of the horoscope (like the Nadir) it tends to turn things upside down. Make sure that Uranus is at least 6° away from the 4th house cusp. Remember that a *conjunction* to the Nadir is also an *opposition* to the Midheaven. When Uranus is placed in the 4th house, it can bring drastic changes to both home and career.

That said, Uranus in the 4th house increases the chances that you will change homes or make changes around the house. The changes are more likely to be on the avant garde side, more daring than you would normally make. As always with Uranus, *don't* make the changes too fast.

Neptune

Neptune in the 4th house is great if you happen to be a poet or a screenwriter, in which case, you can get a lot of work done at home. For the rest of us, it brings daydreaming, flights of fancy, and confusion when we're at home.

Pluto

If you want to do major renovations around the house, Pluto in the 4th house is good. If Pluto is heavily afflicted, look out for troubles with plumbing, insect or rodent infestations, or burglary.

The Nodes

The North Node in the 4th house beneficially focuses your energy towards the home.

The South Node means that you may find home too comfortable and you should focus on career (or at least on things outside of the home) instead. Otherwise, you will be sitting at home unhappily collecting dust-bunnies.

THE FIFTH HOUSE AND ITS PLANETS

The 5th house rules love and romance. Actually, the 5th house also rules children, sports, games, gambling, and speculation. In general, this is the house of *fun*. The 5th house also rules *engagements*. This is the house to concentrate on if you want a relationship. The 7th house rules marriage, but,you need to look at the 5th house since you have to meet them first.

The Sun

The Sun is where the "heart" is. The Sun in the 5th house increases you creativity and your desire to hare fun. The 5th house is the Leo house and, even if you have nothing in Leo in your birth chart, you will find yourself acting in a more dramatic and theatrical fashion with this placement.

The Sun is generally a favorable influence, so the 5th house is a good place to put it if you want to increase you chances in romance, hobbies, sports, etc. However, don't think if you put it here you can go to Las Vegas and bet your life savings at the gaming tables. The odds may improve a bit in your favor, but remember they still favor the house.

This is also a good placement if you want to improve your creativity.

The Moon

The Moon in the 5th house is good for creativity because you can tap into your subconscious more readily. However, you may be moodier in the romantic area. Another possibility is, those you are involved with romantically will be moodier than normal.

Mercury

Mercury in the 5th house is a good placement for creative writing. In the romantic area, it makes for more conversation and can also make you attracted to more than one person at a time.

Venus

Venus in the 5th house can improve romance, but don't expect to meet the love of your life with this placement. The Venus influence is *pleasant* but not dynamic. It makes things work more *smoothly* and you will tend to get along better with romantic partners and children. Fun and games will be more fun. Creativity and artistic ability improve. Just don't expect the Earth to move and the sky to open up.

Mars

Mars is the planet of action, and it does just what you would expect it to do. In the 5th house, Mars will give you action in the romance area. Remember, the fifth house rules more than romance. Mars here is also good for sports and games of all sorts, especially energetic and active ones. If Mars is afflicted, it could mean arguments with either children or romantic interests. Afflicted Mars in the fifth house also cautions you to avoid gambling or speculating.

Jupiter

Jupiter in the 5th house is the placement that worked for Kimberly. Jupiter here helps to expand your romantic life. This placement is also good for sports, games, and having a good time in general. If you are trying to have children, Jupiter is the planet of *expansion*. If you are not trying to have children, remember that Jupiter is also the planet of *overconfidence* ("Oh, we don't need to use birth control tonight"). Remember Jupiter's dual nature if you happen to be gambling or speculating. Yes, it can make you luckier (good). It can also make you overconfident (very bad) and you can blow all your gains.

Saturn

I'm not a doctor and I don't give medical advice, but please don't put Saturn in the 5th house if you are planning to get pregnant. Saturn is the planet of *difficulties, obstacles, and delays.* Being pregnant is tough enough; don't make it worse. If you already have children, they may be giving you more problems, or you become busier and have less time to spend with them. Fortunately, Saturn is also the planet of *organization*, so it will increase your ability to schedule your time. The 5th house also rules gambling. Saturn is "bad" luck. Enough said. Gambling also includes speculation (as in the stock market). Stick to cautious, calculated risks when Saturn is in the 5th house.

Uranus

Uranus in the 5th house is definitely *NOT* dull. Let's put it this way. If you have Uranus in the 5th house, and you go to a party where the majority of the people are *normal*, but there is one "person" there who just got off of a UFO, guess who you are most likely to fall in love with? This is also true if that person is a genius or just escaped from an insane asylum.

Neptune

Neptune in the 5th house is great for creativity, but *watch out* in romance. Neptune is the planet of rose-colored glasses. Wherever it goes, you *see what you want to see*.

Pluto

Pluto in the 5th house is all or nothing. This can be a danger in both sports and romance. In sports and games, you will tend to become more deeply involved. That could be a good thing, but remember that Pluto rules *obsession*. Don't drive yourself over the edge.

The Nodes

The North Node in the 5th house is great for having a good time and enjoying yourself. Romance tends to be better than normal. It will also help you with sports, games, gambling and speculating (watch out, don't push your luck too far) and anything creative. Relations with children can also be improved, mainly because you will have more tolerance for the noise they make.

Forget going to Las Vegas if you have the South Node in the 5th house. Stick to safer investments. Romance and relationships with children can suffer because you are more likely to hover and smother. This drives your loved one away and drives your children crazy.

THE SIXTH HOUSE AND ITS PLANETS

The 6th house is work as opposed to career; i.e. your job. The way you work. The circumstances of health. Don't worry if you put Saturn here. It won't make you sick. This is a *Cadent* house, so it is a good place to put a planet if you want to weaken it. The 6th house also rules subordinates and co-workers and your relationship with them. In more general terms, it shows *service* that you give and receive.

The Sun

The Sun in the 6th house is a good placement if you want to be a workaholic for the next six months.

The Moon

The Moon in the 6th house increases the emotional need to work. It also tends to make you a workaholic. In addition, you may tend to worry *unnecessarily* about your health. Ok, so you may become a raving hypochondriac. No planetary placement is perfect.

Mercury

Mercury in the 6th house is a good placement if you need to get immersed in *details*. If you are the kind of person who gets bogged down in details to begin with, Mercury in the 6th house could make it worse. Mercury is the most easily influenced planet. The 6th house is health. If you hear about some disease, you could easily think that you have it. Yes, this placement also tends to hypochondria.

Venus

Venus in the 6th house is nice for getting along with co-workers and subordinates. Health matters tend to be easier, but watch out for a sudden desire for sweets. Venus rules sugar.

Mars

If you have a lot of work to do, put Mars in the 6th house. Mars is the let's-dive-in-and-get-it-done planet. If Mars is afflicted, be careful of arguments with co-workers or subordinates.

Jupiter

Need a job? Jupiter is the planet of good luck and the 6th house rules employment. Health should be good, but watch out for over-indulgence.

Saturn

No, Saturn in the 6th house does not necessarily mean bad health. If you have a health problem to begin with, Saturn will bring it to the surface so that you can deal with it. However, if you have some sort of chronic condition, Saturn in the 6th house will make it worse. In that case, avoid putting Saturn here.

Not a good placement if you are looking for a new job, unless, of course, you are a masochist who likes hard work, low pay, miserable working conditions, and a cruel boss. If you are already employed, you will be working harder and longer, but remember that Saturn eventually may reward that sort of thing. Watch out though. They may fire someone else and have you do their job as well as your own (and at no additional pay).

If your 2nd house is in good shape, you will get the extra money. If you are self-employed, be sure to pace yourself to avoid working like a dog.

Uranus

Uranus in the 6th house is not dull. You may have a sudden urge to walk out of your job. Literally. This is especially true if the job is *ordinary*. However, Uranus here is very good for any sort of work that is unusual, strange, or shocking. It is also good for hi-tech jobs or anything involving electronics.

In health matters, there is a tendency to get strange illnesses, the kind where the doctor looks at the books and says, "We haven't seen anything like this in twenty years!"

If Uranus is afflicted by Mars, be careful of accidents at work.

Neptune

Neptune in the 6th house is a good placement if your job is creative, or involves film, art, or music. It is also good if you are in the pharmaceutical industry. If Neptune is afflicted, you will have to be careful of confusion or deception on the job. Remember that the 6th house also rules all people who provide you with services. If someone is doing work for you around your house, don't leave them alone. Afflicted Neptune in the 6th house increases the chance of *theft* by servants and employees (as well as by fellow workers).

In health matters, Neptune is the planet of imagination. This increases the likelihood of imaginary illnesses. It also increases the chance of allergies and *sensitivity to drugs* (bad drug reactions).

Medical diagnosis becomes more difficult since Neptune rules fog and confusion. With Uranus, the illnesses are unusual. With Neptune, by the time the doctor figures out what you have, it's already gone.

Pluto

With Pluto in the 6th house, you can become obsessed by your work. This can enable you to accomplish great things. It can also make you collapse from over-exertion. Be careful of power struggles on the job. Pluto rules all things underground, as well as hidden organizations like the Mafia and the Ku Klux Klan. With this placement, co-workers, subordinates, and servants tend to have *hidden agendas*. In other words, they are smiling and telling you how great things will be while they are plotting to screw you royally.

In health matters, Pluto can bring you back from the brink of death. However, it might have been the cause of your being on the brink to begin with! Pluto can make you obsess about the tiniest imperfection in your health (a pimple, for example). On the other hand, you might have some other more serious condition that is hidden. Pluto in the 6th house is therefore a good time to have a complete medical checkup.

The Nodes

The North Node in the 6th house can improve your health and relationships with co-workers and employees. In fact, it improves relationships with anyone who is providing services for you, including clerks in the local store.

Don't hire anyone to renovate your home if you have the South Node in the 6th house. Put it off. The South Node in the 6th house also tends to *hypochondria*.

THE SEVENTH HOUSE AND ITS PLANETS

The 7th house is the house of marriage and partnership. It also rules *open enemies*. Is that a coincidence? I'll let you decide. The 7th house also governs all one-on-one relationships, such as dealings with doctors, lawyers, accountants, and advisors in general.

The Sun

The Sun in the 7th house means partners and partnerships will be a major focus for this time period. The Sun is generally a lucky influence, so it's a good choice to put it here if you want to boost partnership matters. Remember that the 7th house covers more than partnerships. It rules all one-on-one relationships where you and the other person are *equals*. The Sun here can attract people to you who act, well, "Sunny." Cheerful, optimistic, maybe a bit arrogant. At least things won't be dull.

The Moon

The Moon in the 7th house means partnerships will go through constant up and down cycles. Watch out for partners getting moody. Be careful too of your own moodiness towards partners. This placement is not terrible. Just be prepared for some emotional ups and downs.

Mercury

Mercury in the 7th house is great for *communication* with partners. It can also mean a partner who never shuts up.

Venus

Venus in the 7th house tends to smooth relations with partners and has the same effect on one-on-one relationships in general.

Mars

Mars in the 7th house tends to bring you an active partner. It can also bring you lots of arguments with partners. To avoid that, make sure you and your partner are both busy. Yes, lovemaking and passion qualify as keeping busy.

Jupiter

Jupiter in the 7th house can do more for you than merely making marriage and partnerships easier. It increases your contacts which makes it an excellent placement for *networking*. Remember that the 7th house also rules relations with those who provide professional services (i.e. lawyers, doctors, accountants). That makes Jupiter in the 7th house of your return chart a good time period for consultations or looking for new service providers.

By itself, Jupiter in the 7th house won't get you married. But it can improve things for you if you are already married. Your partner will tend to be more "Jovial." Be careful though. Jupiter can also mean over-optimism. Everything looks great until the next return chart when Jupiter is no longer there. That's when you say, "What was I thinking?" and head for divorce court.

Saturn

No, Saturn in the 7th house does not mean a certain divorce. Amateurs frequently jump to this wrong conclusion. Jupiter can get you into a bad marriage because it makes you over optimistic. Saturn can stop you from making a big mistake. If your marriage or business partnership is on the rocks, Saturn will tell you in no uncertain terms that you have to deal with the problems or it's all over.

I had a client once who had a husband AND a boyfriend. Transiting Saturn was approaching her 7th house. That is similar to having Saturn in the 7th house of a return chart. In the case of transits though, there is no way to avoid it. I told her that she would have to make a decision. She told me she didn't want to make a decision, that she liked things just the way they were. Two weeks after Saturn hit, both relationships abruptly ended.

She suddenly decided she couldn't stand her husband any more, so she walked out on him. A couple of days later, her very conservative lawyer boyfriend announced he was marrying a rock singer.

The moral of this story is *NEVER* let Saturn make decisions for you.

Uranus

I had Uranus in the 7th house in 1985 when I met my now ex-wife. Coinsidentally, she had Uranus in the 7th house in her birthday chart as well. She left her fiancé, sold her business, moved to New York, and married me. The marriage ended suddenly just a few months later. I learned a lot about relationship astrology from that experience. What Uranus gets together quickly, it can break apart just as quickly.

Remember that the 7th house also rules business partnerships, so be careful in that department too.

If you are married or living with someone and Uranus is here, give each other plenty of *SPACE*. Uranus is big on being independent and doing your own thing. If it doesn't get that space, Uranus will push you further apart.

Neptune

Try not to start a new marriage or partnership with Neptune in the 7th house. There will be a very strong tendency to see what you want to see. You don't find out until later that the person you thought was your soul mate is really an alcoholic, drug abuser, con-artist, ex-convict, bigamist, or someone who just got out of the insane asylum. You may also discover that your partner's sexual orientation was not what you originally thought.

If you are already married (or living with someone) or in a business partnership, be careful of confusion and misunderstandings. This also applies to dealings with professional advisors. You are more likely to receive bad advice now, but usually this is merely confusion. Double check to make sure that the doctor told you to take that medicine every four hours and not twice a day. This advice also applies if you are consulting an astrologer!

Pluto

With Pluto in the 7th house things probably won't be dull. Make sure Pluto isn't too close to the beginning of the 7th house. That point is called the Descendant, and it is one of the strong points of the horoscope. Pluto making a conjunction to the Descendant can bring major arguments and battles.

The Nodes

The North Node in the 7th house can improve relations with partners, but watch out. It can also give you the desire for the *perfect partner* (and there ain't no such thing). You will have to stifle an urge to *improve* the partner. Please don't try to change them.

The South Node in the 7th house can make you think that a committed relationship will fix your entire life. Dream on. With this placement, you can start projects with others but, at a critical point, they will not be available (they may desert you) and you will have to finish up by yourself. On the positive side, your open enemies can suddenly go out of your life.

THE EIGHTH HOUSE AND ITS PLANETS

The 8th house is the house of sex, death, rebirth, and credit. That's an interesting combination. The 8th house also rules *other people's money* in general. This is the house to concentrate on if you're having credit problems or if you want to improve resources you own jointly with a partner.

The Sun

No, the Sun in the 8th house does not mean you, or the people around you, are going to die. You can't kill someone else by adjusting your own birthday horoscope. If that were possible, a lot more people would be consulting astrologers ("Where do I go to get rid of my mother-in-law?").

What an 8th house Sun may do is improve your credit rating, help you in all matters concerning inheritance and insurance, make rehabilitation easier, and (last but not least) give a boost to your sex life. If the Sun is strongly afflicted, you are likely to have trouble in those areas.

The Moon

The Moon in the 8th house shows our instincts, emotional needs, and subconscious urges. Watch out for a sudden urge to spend with credit cards. Your sex life will tend to be more subject to mood swings. Instincts can be a good thing, but check them first with a little logical analysis. That can save you a lot of grief.

Mercury

Mercury in the 8th house is a good position to have if you write murder mysteries. It's also excellent if you are a psychologist or therapist, since you are dealing with 8th house matters. Ditto if you are an accountant. Mercury here will help you deal more effectively with your client's accounts.

Venus

Venus always makes things smoother and easier and is no different in the 8th house. Sex will tend to be more pleasant. Insurance, credit, and inheritance matters should give you fewer problems with Venus here.

Mars

Mars in the 8th house can be good for the more physical side of sex. Mars is the planet of action, so make sure both you and your partner are in good physical shape. Be careful with your credit card spending. Mars is action and the 8th house is *other people's money*. Avoid making major purchases on credit. You will tend to pay too much now because you are more impulsive.

Jupiter

I only have two cases where I sent people traveling to put Jupiter in the 8th house. Both were for financial reasons. The first one had a terrible credit rating and she needed a new credit card. She got a new card a few weeks after she returned, but she complained to me that she also had a lot of one-night-stands. She was smiling when she complained, so I didn't think she minded too much.

The other case was the teenage daughter of a client. She was going to college and needed financial aid. I sent her to Chicago to put Jupiter in the 8th house. Her mother reported that she did get a combination of grants and loans (both of which are ruled by the 8th house) which paid for her educational expenses. A month later, the daughter called to tell me that she just had her first sexual experience. So if you want luck with other people's money, be aware of this side effect. You may get lucky in another sense.

Saturn

Don't put Saturn in the 8th house if you need a loan or are expecting an inheritance. Remember that Saturn increases the chance of *delays*. In matters of sex, Saturn can mean *less*, mostly because you are busy with something else. However, Saturn also rules leather and bondage. I leave the rest to your imagination. This is not a good placement if you are undergoing any sort of rehabilitation, mainly because of the increased delays and obstacles.

Uranus

Uranus in the 8th house can add spice to your sex life. I call this the "But honey, we did the chandeliers last night" placement. As far as inheritance, credit, and insurance are concerned, expect the unexpected. If Uranus is well aspected, the sudden changes will tend to be in your favor. If it is afflicted, watch out.

Uranus well aspected in the 8th house is generally good for new or experimental methods of rehabilitation. The opposite is true if Uranus is afflicted. Again, I am not a medical doctor and this is *not* to be interpreted as medical advice. This is just a general tendency of the influence of Uranus.

Neptune

With Neptune in the 8th house, you are more easily seducible, especially when there is alcohol around. Two glasses of wine is all it will take to make you *dangerous*. Avoid running up your credit cards if Neptune lands here. On the other hand, if you have to raise money for business purposes, this placement makes it easier because you can paint a beautiful picture to investors.

Pluto

Since Pluto is extremes, a placement in the 8th house can mean either fantastic, intense sexual experiences or a desire for celibacy. Remember that Pluto doesn't get you a sexual partner. All it does is increase your desires. If there's nobody around, this can make you very, very frustrated.

The Nodes

The North Node in the 8th house is good for matters of inheritance and insurance, as well as partnership finances. Sex will tend to be better too. Remember though, the 8th house does not *get* you a romantic partner. That's the job of the 5th house. But once you have one, the 8th house goes to work. Make sure you're in good physical shape though. In fact, make sure your romantic partner is in good physical shape too. Have fun.

With the South Node in the 8th house, payments from insurance, inheritance, and loans from others will tend to be delayed. This can also delay probate of wills. Watch out if you are buying insurance. It is very easy to get royally screwed with this one. Do not believe what the insurance agent says (you shouldn't anyway, but especially so with this placement). Read the policy very, very carefully.

Sex, with the South Node in the 8th house, is like a restaurant I once went to. They served plenty of food, but it wasn't good.

Since the 8th house also rules the values of those around you, be careful not to be too easily influenced by others. It is more important at this time to use your own judgment and strengthen your own values. It can also mean that you are trying to push your values on to others. It won't work now. Let them go their own way.

THE NINTH HOUSE AND ITS PLANETS

The 9th house governs long journeys (trips where you have to stay overnight), higher education, in-laws, religious matters, and lawsuits. I have had a lot of disagreements with other astrologers about this. Many of them look to the 7th house for legal disputes. However, in my experience, the 7th house (open enemies) will only show your opposition. The lawsuit itself is shown by the 9th house.

Why does the 9th house rules in-laws? First of all, it is opposite the 3rd house (brothers and sisters) so it shows the marriage partners of your siblings. But how about the brothers and sisters of your marriage partner? Your marriage partner is shown by the 7th house so their siblings are shown by their third house. To find their third house, put your finger on the 7th house and count counter-clockwise. Guess where you wind up. That's right, the 9th house again. So the 9th house also rules the brothers and sisters of your marriage partner.

The 9th house also rules publishing.

If you're having troubles with in-laws, higher education, legal matters, publishing, or long trips, this is the house you have to work on.

The Sun

The Sun in the 9th house is a good placement if you are going to take a long journey or enter a course of higher education. It is also beneficial for legal matters and all other 9th house matters.

The Moon

The Moon in the 9th house gives an *emotional need* to take a long journey or to study something. If you can't actually travel or take a course, at least read about a subject that interests you or about far-off places. You may find yourself attracted on an emotional level to foreigners or people from backgrounds very different from yours.

Mercury

Mercury in the 9th house is a good placement for higher education. Mercury is the planet of communication, so putting it here makes learning easier. It can also be helpful with legal matters, such as filing briefs, and helpful with travel.

Venus

Venus tends to make things easier and more pleasant. Venus in the 9th house is a good placement for long-distance pleasure trips. Legal matters are eased. Venus here makes it more likely that out-of-court settlements will be reached instead of having battles in front of a judge. Higher education can also proceed more smoothly. This is a good placement if you want to study music or art.

Mars

No question about it. If you are going to travel to a distant place or take a course, Mars in the 9th house will give you the energy to do it. In the legal area, you will tend to have increased desire for battle, but watch out! You could be fighting in court when it would be better to settle. Don't get carried away.

Jupiter

Juptier in the 9th house can give *luck* with all 9th house matters. It is certainly favorable for legal matters and publishing. If Jupiter is afflicted though, it can easily lead to overconfidence.

Saturn

No, Saturn in the 9th house is not always a disaster. In fact, if you have no legal matters and you are not going to publish anything, this can be a nice out-of-the-way placement for this *Greater Malefic*. In legal matters, it can cause delays, at the very least. Expect delays too, with long journeys. This is not the place to put Saturn if you are taking a long-distance pleasure trip, although it is okay for business trips.

Uranus

Uranus in the 9th house is a good placement for studying any subject that is new, unusual, strange, or just plain not socially acceptable. I wouldn't put it here if you had legal troubles. Uranus can be very unpredictable.

Neptune

Neptune in the 9th house is good for studying any subject that requires creativity and imagination. Subjects like accounting are not so favored. It can also make you more likely to dream of traveling to a tropical island. If you are an author, this placement can cause extra confusion with your publisher. There is also confusion with legal matters. If you are suing someone (or being sued) avoid putting Neptune here.

Pluto

The 9th is one of the *cadent houses*. These are weaker, out-of-the-way areas of the horoscope, so they are a good place to put planets that can be dangerous, like Pluto. Pluto is the planet of extremes, death and rebirth. Yes, it may change the principles you live by and your view of the Universe, but this is rare. If you are involved in a lawsuit, you may become obsessed with beating your opponent. Conversely, they may be obsessed with beating you.

If you're taking a long trip, try to go to a place that has volcanic soil (or better still, a live volcano!) or archeological ruins. These are ruled by Pluto and the trip will be much more fascinating.

If Pluto happens to make a lot of stress aspects, or if it is making stress aspects to planets in your natal chart, put it in this house and then *AVOID* taking long trips and getting involved in lawsuits.

The Nodes

The North Node in the 9th house indicates you should concentrate more on getting the big picture. Avoid the tendency to get bogged down in day-to-day details. This will be a good time period to plan ahead. Since the North Node acts like a little Jupiter, it tends to make all 9th house matters easier. Just remember that the planets in the 9th house and the ruling planet of the sign on the house cusp have greater importance.

With the South Node in the 9th, you may find long journeys draining. Be careful for a tendency to stay in college longer than you have to just because you find it easier than graduating and getting a job.

THE TENTH HOUSE AND ITS PLANETS

The 10th house is career and public "image." The effect of the planet will be magnified if it is also within 6° of the Midheaven. The closer it is, the stronger the impact.

The Sun

The Sun in the 10th house can get you noticed (especially if the Sun is making a conjunction with the Midheaven).

The Moon

The Moon in the 10th house can bring you more notice than the Sun since the Moon rules the public. Make sure the Moon is well aspected though; otherwise it could give you a different type of public *acclaim*, a type you might not like.

Mercury

With Mercury in the 10th house, people will talk about you and about what you do. What they say will depend on the nature of the aspects to Mercury.

Venus

With Venus in the 10th house, you and what you do will *look good*. The only real danger from Venus in the 10th house is that it may make you lazier. If so, enjoy it!

Mars

Mars in the 10th house worked for me the first time I traveled for my birthday. Mars is action. Whatever else your career may be, it won't be dull. You will be more likely to dive right in and get things done. Watch out for arguments with bosses.

Jupiter

A well-aspected Jupiter in the 10th house will tend to expand your career. This is especially good if you are in show business because you need all the luck you can get.

Saturn

Saturn in the 10th house is a really great placement to have if you are a masochist and want to make things tougher for yourself. You'll have an uphill battle in your career, and your boss will like you less (probably a lot less). The 10th house rules all authority figures, so if you're in court, don't expect a break from the judge.

Uranus

If Uranus is in the 10th house, make sure it's not making a close conjunction to the Midheaven. Uranus here is a great placement to have if you like getting fired suddenly and without warning. It's also good if you want to quit your job for no apparent reason. Your job can also end with your company suddenly going out of business. On the other hand, this is a good placement to have if you are unemployed and there are no prospects on the horizon. Uranus is like a defibrillator. You use it in an emergency, when someone's heart stops. But it's not something you use everyday or in normal circumstances.

As long as Uranus is not close to the Midheaven, this is an okay placement if you want to liven up your career or public image. Uranus in the 10th house can make you see new opportunities and different ways of doing things.

Neptune

Neptune in the 10th house is good if you happen to be in the movie industry or if you have to project an *image* to the public. It is also good for any career that requires imagination or creativity. In addition, it is helpful for any career that requires compassion, such as social work or the healing professions.

Pluto

If Pluto is in the 10th house, try to make sure that it is not on the Midheaven (within a 6° orb). Doing that could be dangerous for your career and public image. The only time to have Pluto making a conjunction with your Midheaven is if your career is *dead* and has no prospects of coming back. In that case, there is a chance that Pluto may bring it back to life. If you like your career and public image, keep Pluto away from your Midheaven. Remember that it is the planet of death.

If Pluto is in the 10th house but not near the Midheaven, the following six months will be a good time to re-examine your career, to ask who you are and where you're going with your life. You will still have to be careful of potential power struggles with your boss, parents, and authority figures in general. If you're ambitious, this can increase it to the point of obsession.

The Nodes

The North Node in the 10th house means extra luck with career matters and dealing with bosses.

If the South Node is in the 10th house, now is not a good time to ask for a raise.

THE ELEVENTH HOUSE AND ITS PLANETS

Most books tell you that the 11th house is the house of *friends, hopes and wishes*. What they usually don't say is that it also rules money that you get directly from career; it is the 2nd house from the 10th. In addition, the 11th house shows your relations with *groups* of people. This is the house to strengthen if you are planning to do a lot of *business socializing*. Socializing for *fun* is ruled by the 5th house.

The Sun

The Sun in the 11th house is a good placement if you need to gain the favor of powerful people. It's also good for getting the rewards from a successful career. It is an excellent placement if you are dealing with groups of people and you need to attract attention and favor.

The Moon

The Moon in the 11th house is good for relationships with female friends and with women in power. Remember that the Moon is *moody and changeable*. If you have this placement in your return chart and a friend offers you a deal, you have to make up your mind right away and tell them your answer *immediately*. Otherwise, they are likely to change their mind a short time later.

Mercury

Mercury in the 11th house is a great placement for *networking* and business communications.

Venus

Venus in the 11th house is good for socializing and networking. Venus here tends to make relations with friends *smoother*. It also makes the time you spend with friends more fun.

Mars

No, Mars in the 11th house does *not* necessarily mean you're going to fight with friends. Usually it makes for more *action* in friendships. Instead of sitting around and talking, you are more likely to be out and about. This is a good placement for sporting activities with friends. In business dealings with groups, you will tend to be more assertive now. If Mars is afflicted, take care that you don't come on too strong.

Jupiter

Jupiter in the 11th house is a good placement to have if you want to expand your circle of friends. It is also excellent for contact with rich and powerful people. The downside for Jupiter here is you may neglect the details necessary to achieve your hopes and wishes.

Saturn

If Saturn is in the 11th house, you'll most likely be spending less time with friends. Either you or they will be busier than usual. Conversations with friends will tend to be about serious subjects. Saturn here can reduce the number of friends you have by taking them away from you one way or another. It can also take away some of your hopes and wishes, especially the unrealistic ones.

Uranus

Uranus in the 11th house means *excitement!* Well, that's true wherever Uranus goes. This is the planet that likes to overturn the applecart. Uranus here is good for making exciting new friends or joining new and stimulating groups.

Neptune

Be careful listening to friends when Neptune is in the 11th house. Their advice may be imaginative and fascinating, but it won't be too realistic. In some cases, it could be delusional, inappropriate, and even deceptive. Most of the time, it is just plain wrong. In business, you run the risk of losses because you will tend to neglect important details.

Pluto

Pluto in the 11th house can give you powerful friends... and enemies. With this placement, you could be obsessed with achieving your hopes and wishes, so make sure you're wishing for the right things.

The Nodes

The North Node in the 11th house can give benefits obtained through friends; in fact, friendships are enhanced. The South Node in the 11th house means you should concentrate less on friends and more on your own creativity and enjoyment. If you have any friends you have outgrown, the South Node placed here will let you know it.

THE TWELFTH HOUSE AND ITS PLANETS

If you want a planet to be out of the way and not have too much of an effect, this is the place to put it.

WARNING: If the planet is a **malefic**, make sure it is more than 6° from the Ascendant. It also helps if it is in a **different sign** than the Ascendant.

The 12th house rules *hidden enemies* and *self-destructive behavior*. A planet close to the Ascendant and *in the same sign* can show a hidden enemy suddenly coming out of the woodwork and attacking you.

If you need to be noticed in your work (if you are in show business, for instance) do not put the planet that rules the Midheaven here. No one will notice you for six months. You might as well be invisible.

The Sun

Try not to put the Sun in the 12th house. This placement lowers your stamina, increases your chance of depression, and makes you much less visible. If you're in show business, avoid this placement like the plague. No one will notice you, and, even more, no one will care.

On the other hand, if you work in a prison or a hospital, this placement is not bad. In that environment, it will help you to get along.

The Moon

With the Moon in the 12th house, watch out for depression. The 12th house is *hidden things*. In this case, it is your emotions that become invisible. No one will know or care what you are feeling, and they will tend to be annoyed when you express any emotion at all. On the other hand, if you're living in a hostile environment (or if you're a spy) and have to keep your true feelings hidden, this placement can help.

The Moon in the 12th house is good if you are planning a divorce or you are getting ready to leave an unpleasant job. It will help you to conceal your true feelings while you plot your escape.

Mercury

With Mercury in the 12th house, no one will listen to you. Your words fall on deaf ears. However, this position is good if you have a lot of writing to do. You can go off all by yourself (12th house) and write your great novel.

Venus

When Venus is in the 12th house, our affections will be invisible, or, even worse, unimportant. This is a placement for *unrequited love*. The object of your affections barely knows you exist. If you are an artist, no one will see what you produce.

Mars

If well aspected, Mars in the 12th house can give you energy for working behind the scenes. This is a perfect placement if you are plotting the overthrow of a tyrant. Boy are you *ANGRY!!!* Mars here can hide and suppress the anger. If it comes out all at once, it can do so explosively and destructively. If the anger doesn't come out at all, it can cause all sorts of bodily ailments.

Jupiter

Jupiter can give you luck wherever it goes. In the 12th house, it will protect you from *hidden enemies*. Nevertheless, this is not the best place to put Jupiter. It's the house of restriction, and who wants to restrict their luck?

Saturn

Saturn in the 12th house is a good placement because it is the planet of *difficulties, obstacles, and delays*. Here, it is out of the way and less likely to bother you. If you are depressed, no one will notice or care. Be very careful though not to put Saturn close to the Ascendant. In that case, it will mean hidden enemies will come out of the woodwork. You will feel this and dread it, but you won't know where the unknown disaster will be coming from.

Saturn in the 12th house can also make it more likely that you will be visiting someone who is confined.

Uranus

Uranus in the 12th house tends to make your thinking shaky and inconsistent. This is definitely *NOT* the time to show your new invention to the public. If Uranus here is close to the Ascendant, your life will be filled with unpleasant surprises, including *accidents*. If Uranus is deep enough in the 12th house, you won't have to worry about the accidents and surprises, but you will still have to watch out for a tendency to change your mind every two minutes.

Neptune

The 12th house is Neptune's natural house. With this placement, imagination and creativity get a big boost. An excellent placement for musicians and dancers. Be careful of an excessive amount of daydreaming. This placement is also popular with dope smokers.

Again, make sure Neptune is not close to the Ascendant; keep it at least 6° away. It is also best to make sure that Neptune is not in the same sign as the Ascendant. If Neptune is within 6° of the Ascendant and in the same sign, you will be highly prone to *deception*.

Pluto

Pluto in the 12th house can make you dwell on the seamier side of life. Pluto in the 12th house can make your therapist rich because all sorts of things get dredged up from your subconscious. Never put a 12th house Pluto close to the Ascendant. This one can attract the nastiest hidden enemies you can imagine. You will tend to see hidden threats everywhere. Although the things you see are real, they are not threats. Pluto simply makes you overreact.

The Nodes

The North Node in the 12th house can protect you from enemies. If the North Node is close to the Ascendant, it will cause your enemies to "melt away" and disappear. This is also a good placement for figuring out your next move and planning your future.

The South Node in the 12th house can make you lazy. If it is close to your Ascendant, it will drain you and give power to your enemies.

Astrology Terminology

Angular *See* Houses.

ascendant Also called the Rising Sign. This is the beginning of the 1st house. The Ascendant shows your outward traits, the traits that people are most likely to notice when first meeting you.

aspects Aspects are certain angles between planets in the horoscope. They were originally classified into "good" and "bad" aspects. Today we know that "bad" aspects can sometimes have really good effects. Many astrologers now call the bad aspects "stressful" or challenging."

benefics (greater & lesser) Planets with an allegedly "benefic" influence. Jupiter is the greater benefic (but it can also make you fat). Venus is the lesser benefic (it can make you lazy too).

Cadent *See* Houses.

Chart, Birth *See* Chart, Natal.

Chart, Birthday *See* Return, Solar.

Chart, Natal Also called the Birth Chart. This is the horoscope calculated for the exact moment of birth. For people, this is the time of the first breath. Horoscopes can be calculated for any event as long as we know the exact time.

cusp A "cusp" is the beginning of a house. A planet is "on the cusp" if it is right at that point.

Descendant The point opposite the Ascendant. This is the beginning of the 7th house. The Ascendant shows our outward traits. The Descendant shows our relations with others on an equal, one-to-one basis. Interestingly enough, this area of the horoscope shows both marriage partners and open enemies (since we tend to treat both as equals).

GRAND TRINE Three planets making an equilateral triangle in the horoscope. Said to be beneficial, but it can make a person too satisfied with themselves so they never try to change anything.

HOUSES The twelve divisions of the horoscope wheel. Houses are divided into three groups. The *angular* houses are 1, 4, 7, and 10. These show how you start things. The *succedent* houses are 2, 5, 8, and 11. These houses succeed the angular houses and they show how you develop and expand the things you started in the angular houses. The *cadent* houses are 3, 6, 9, and 12. These are mental houses and govern communication. You can look at cadent houses in two ways. They precede the angular houses, so you could say thought comes before action. They follow the succedent houses, so you could also say that once things have been started and developed, you sit around and think about them. Thinking can lead to new possibilities (what if?) and this eventually leads to more action and new beginnings. That brings us back to the angular houses and the cycle begins again.

MALEFICS Planets with an allegedly bad influence. Mars is the lesser malefic (but without it, there would be no energy to get anything done). Saturn is the greater malefic (without obstacles, there would be no growth).

MIDHEAVEN The sign and degree that is at the "highest" point of the horoscope. This is the beginning of the 10th house. Technically, it is where the ecliptic (the Sun's apparent path across the sky) hits the Prime Meridian.

MOON The Moon always shows one's emotions and instincts. The location of the Moon in a return chart shows where our feelings are focused for the time period of the return, what we are emotionally drawn to during that time. In addition, the Moon's location is the place where we will be likely to change our mind and reverse course. We don't call it "the Inconstant Moon" for nothing.

NADIR The bottom of the horoscope. This is the point opposite the Midheaven. It is the beginning of the 4th house, which rules the home.

RETROGRADE All planets sometimes seem to be moving backwards. The effect is similar to looking out of a moving car and noticing that slower traffic seems to backing up. Retrograde motion can slightly weaken the effect of a planet.

RETURN, LUNAR A horoscope calculated for the exact moment the Moon returns to the exact place it occupied when you were born. Since the Earth's orbit also moves around the Sun, this location changes a little bit every year.

RETURN, SOLAR Also called the "birthday horoscope," this horoscope calculated for the exact moment the Sun apparently "returns" to the location it occupied when you were born. Since the Earth's orbit also moves around the Sun, this location changes a little bit every year.

SUCCEDENT *See* Houses.

Chart illustrations

www.BobMarksAstrologer.com

CPSIA information can be obtained at www.ICGtesting.com
Printed in the USA
BVOW02s0828040116

431641BV00002B/59/P